REPORT WRITING

ESSENTIALS

EASY TO UNDERSTAND

- *Grammar*
- *Punctuation*
- *Spelling*
- *Sentence Structure*
- *Sample Reports*
- *Exercises*

Lance A. Parr

Copperhouse
@
ATOMICdogPUBLISHING

COPPERHOUSE PUBLISHING COMPANY
P.O. Box 5463, Incline Village, Nevada 89450

All Copperhouse titles are now distributed by
Atomic Dog Publishing

Atomic Dog is a higher education publishing company that specializes in developing and publishing HyBred Media™ textbooks that combine online content delivery, interactive media, and print. You may contact Atomic Dog as follows:

1203 Main Street, Fifth Floor
Cincinnati, OH 45210
800.310.5661, ext. 12   Fax 513.333.0498
e-mail copperhouse@atomicdog.com
www.atomicdog.com

Your Partner in Education
with
QUALITY BOOKS AT FAIR PRICES

Library of Congress Catalog Number 91-70495
ISBN 0-942728-99-8 Paper Text Edition

4 5 6 7 8 9 10

Printed in the United States of America.

TABLE OF CONTENTS

Nouns defined, Examples, Practice
Specific and vague nouns defined, Examples, Practice
Collective nouns defined, Examples, Practice
Pronouns defined, Examples, Practice
Possessive pronouns defined, Examples, Practice
Indefinite and confusing pronouns, Examples, Practice

Regular and irregular verbs defined, Examples, Practice
Verb tense defined, Examples, Practice
First person sentence construction defined, Examples, Practice
Sentence subject defined, Examples, Practice
Subject-verb agreement defined, Examples, Practice
Pronoun-antecedent defined, Examples, Practice

Adjectives defined, Examples, Practice
Adverbs defined, Examples, Practice
Modifiers defined, Examples, Practice
Comparative modifiers defined, Examples, Practice
Confusing modifiers explained, Examples, Practice
Complete sentences defined, Examples, Practice
Run-on sentences defined, Examples, Practice
Comma splice defined, Examples, Practice

Punctuation effect explained, Examples, Practice
Comma usage explained, Examples, Practice
Apostrophe usage explained, Examples Practice
Forming possessives explained, Examples, Practice
Parentheses, brackets, dashes, hyphens, colons, semi-colons,
Quotation marks, underlining and italics usage explained, Examples, Practice

APPENDICES

ABOUT THE AUTHOR...

Lance Parr is uniquely qualified to write this book. He has a Bachelor of Arts degree in English and a Master of Arts degree in education. He is one of very few people who has served over fifteen years with state, county *and* city law enforcement agencies.

Mr. Parr holds *dan* (black belt) ranking in three different martial arts. He has been a licensed private investigator and a certified firearms instructor for security personnel. At various times he has been a consultant to the California Commission on Peace Officer Standards and Training (POST) and the Correctional Peace Officer Standards and Training Commission of California (CPOST).

For the past several years, Mr. Parr has taught semester-length courses in report writing and criminal justice at Grossmont College in California, where he is a Professor in the Administration of Justice Program.

FOREWORD

Report Writing Essentials meets and exceeds *all* performance objectives for police report writing prescribed by the California commission of Peace Officer Standards and Training (POST) for the basic academy course. It does so by dealing with a broad range of police report writing problems which have been specifically identified by extensive research and empirical data as being the greatest cause of confusing police reports.

Report Writing Essentials was formerly entitled *Police Report Writing Essentials.* The slight change in the name reflects the changes you will find throughout this second edition. Whereas the former text and title was appropriate for use by police agencies of every sort, this new edition has been modified for use by all practitioners of public safety including correctional officers and private security personnel. Although laws may vary from state to state, the tenets of good written public safety communication do not. *Clear, understandable written communication in a public safety report is what this text is all about.*

To aid student leaning, each topic is presented in an easy-to-understand, step-by-step format. Each topic is followed by a practice exercise. Answers to all practices are found in Appendix A to provide students with immediate feedback.

Examples of poor and good police reports are provided in Appendix B. A glossary of grammar, punctuation and other English composition terms (with examples) is provided in Appendix C. The text also includes a list of commonly misspelled words frequently found in public safety reports.

There are no grammar or punctuation exercises without purposes in this book. Grammar and composition rules not directly applicable to public safety reports were purposely excluded in order to make this a *practical*, practice-oriented text on the *essentials* of good public safety report writing.

CHAPTER 1

NOUNS AND PRONOUNS

PERFORMANCE OBJECTIVES – After studying this chapter, you will be able to:

➤   Identify nouns and properly use them in sentences.

➤   Identify vague nouns and change them to specific nouns.

➤   Identify collective nouns and properly use them in sentences.

➤   Identify pronouns and properly use them in sentences.

➤   Identify possessive pronouns in sentences.

➤   Use the pronoun *myself* correctly.

➤   Identify indefinite pronouns and properly use them in sentences.

➤   Modify sentences or pronouns to eliminate confusing pronouns.

Before we begin studying nouns and pronouns, your unspoken question deserves an answer. That question is, I'll bet, **what has this got to do with public safety work?** Everyone knows that public safety personnel must write reports. Perhaps you do *not* know that one of the biggest needs in public safety is better report writing. *Why?*

You see, the catching and securing of crooks is not the problem. Cops, security officers and correctional officers do a pretty good job of that. *Keeping* them caught and safely secure is another matter. How do you keep crooks caught and safely secure? You see to it they are convicted, charged with custody rules violations, and convicted again if they break laws while in custody. You revoke their probation and parole. How do you do that? You see to it that prosecutors issue complaints instead of dropping charges. You see to it that prosecutors do not accept plea bargains to lesser charges that only vaguely resemble what you caught the crooks doing. You make them follow custody rules and conditions of probation and parole. How do you do *that?* Since the entire criminal justice system rides on a sea of paper, you must have the skills necessary for effective public safety written communications!

Your next most likely question is **why start with nouns? Didn't I learn enough about them in the third grade?** The answer is, I'm afraid, yes and no. Yes, you learned about nouns in the third grade. No, you probably did not learn about subject-verb agreement there. Many of you either *never* learned about subject-verb agreement or you forgot what you learned.

Subject-verb agreement (which will be defined later) is a public safety written communications problem. Poor subject-verb agreement can lead to poor communication and *that* can lead to crooks beating the system. *Before understanding subject-verb agreement you will need to understand its component parts.* **Nouns are component parts of subject-verb agreement.**

Nouns are words for places, things, people, ideas and states of mind.

EXAMPLES

He was booked in the **jail**. *(jail is a noun for a place)*

The **bicycle** was stolen. *(bicycle is a noun for a thing)*

Jim is very courteous. *(Jim is a noun for a person)*

Justice should be served. *(justice is a noun for an idea)*

I am **ready** for duty. *(ready is a noun for a state of mind)*

PRACTICE 1.1

DIRECTIONS: Underline all the nouns in each sentence. There may be more than one noun in each sentence.

1. Sam gave the evidence to Frank.
2. George got the knife from Larry.
3. Bob is a good officer.
4. The burglar was mad but decided to tell the truth anyway.

(The answers for all practices are given in Appendix A)

Nouns can be specific or vague. **In public safety reports you should use the most specific nouns for which you have factual information.**

EXAMPLES

The suspect has a **weapon**. *(Very vague—includes catapults, blow guns, knives and cannons)*

The suspect has a **firearm**. *(Less vague than **weapon**, but still includes everything from cannons to flintlock pistols)*

The suspect has a **pistol**. *(Somewhat specific but still includes all revolvers, semi-automatic pistols, derringers and black powder pistols)*

Of course, if you only know that the suspect was armed with a pistol (as opposed to a bow-and-arrow) you should only state that in your report.

PRACTICE 1.2

DIRECTIONS: Underline the most specific nouns from each pair of nouns in parentheses.

1. The (vehicle, truck) was blue.
2. The (assault, shooting) took place on Main Street.
3. The (male, man) wore a blue shirt.
4. His (person, breath) smelled like an alcoholic beverage.

Collective nouns name a number of persons or things as a single group. You will need to be able to identify collective nouns later when dealing with subject-verb agreement.

EXAMPLES

The **jury** delivered a guilty verdict. *(There are many people in a jury, but a jury is a single thing.)*

The **mob** looted the store. *(There's no such thing as a mob consisting of one person, but a mob is a single thing composed of many people.)*

PRACTICE 1.3

DIRECTIONS: Underline the collective nouns.

1. Members of the teenage gang interrupted the party.
2. He shot into the crowd of shoppers.
3. The motorcycle club included several ex-felons.
4. The traffic jam caused numerous accidents.

Pronouns are component parts of subject-verb agreement and, if misused, can add confusion to public safety reports. **A pronoun is a word that takes the place of a noun.**

EXAMPLES

The suspect lost **his** gun. (**His** takes the place of **suspect** so you do not have to write: The suspect lost the suspect's gun.)

I lost **my** flashlight.

PRACTICE 1.4

DIRECTIONS: Underline the pronouns. There may be more than one pronoun in each sentence.

1. He asked his younger sister to watch them for him.
2. They said those were the suspect's pants.
3. You are the first to use it.
4. He said he had seized them as evidence.

Possessive pronouns show ownership *without the use of apostrophes*.

EXAMPLES

They were **his** handcuffs.

Theirs was the newest car.

PRACTICE 1.5

DIRECTIONS: Underline the possessive pronouns. There may be more than one possessive pronoun in each sentence.

1. Ours is better than yours.
2. The knife used in the murder was hers.

Pronouns change depending on their uses in sentences.

EXAMPLES

Jones and **I** arrested the drunk driver.

The drunk driver gave **me** a struggle.

My partner is Smith.

In each of the above examples the pronoun refers to the writer. Deciding which pronoun to use can be confusing. Instead of memorizing rules on correct pronoun usage, leave out the confusing parts of sentences and **listen** for what sounds correct.

EXAMPLE

Jones and _____ arrested the drunk driver. Leave out "Jones and ..." Now try to find the correct pronoun for this sentence: "_____ arrested the drunk driver." **Me** arrested the drunk driver? No. **My** arrested the drunk driver? No. Only "**I** arrested the drunk driver" sounds right. Therefore, "Jones and **I** arrested the drunk driver" is correct.

PRACTICE 1.6

DIRECTIONS: Underline the correct pronouns in parentheses.

1. Tom and (she, her) saw the marijuana plants.
2. My partner and (I, me) made three arrests last week.
3. The two suspects, Smith and (she, her) were at the house.
4. (He, Him) and I will take that call right away.

Use the pronoun *myself* only in the phrase *by myself* or after the pronouns *I* or *me*. It is usually not needed but may be used for emphasis.

EXAMPLES:

Acceptable: I, myself, signed the affidavit.

Acceptable: I did it by **myself.**

Acceptable: I had the place all to **myself.**

Incorrect: Myself and Bill went to court.

Also incorrect: Bill and **myself** went to court

PRACTICE 1.7

DIRECTIONS: Underline the correct pronoun from each pair in parentheses.

1. Tom and (myself, I) went to the suspect's house together.
2. The accident was seen by Parker and (me, myself).

Indefinite pronouns are words that refer to indefinite or undetermined numbers of people or things. You will need to understand indefinite pronouns later when dealing with subject-verb agreement.

EXAMPLES

> **Everybody** had a good time. *(It cannot be determined from this sentence how many people had a good time.)*
>
> **Anyone** might have done the same thing.

PRACTICE 1.8

> **DIRECTIONS:** Underline the indefinite pronouns.
>
> 1.   He knows something.
> 2.   Everyone was in complete agreement.
> 3.   He was willing to sell to anyone who asked.
> 4.   Anybody could have seen it.

If you use a pronoun, it must be clear which noun it is replacing.

EXAMPLES

> **Confusing:** The officer told Adams that **he** had made a mistake. *(To whom does **he** refer? The officer? Adams?)*
>
> **More clear:** The officer made a mistake. **He** told Sgt. Adams.
>
> **Confusing:** The car chased the motorcycle until **it** got a flat tire. *(To which vehicle does **it** refer? The car? The motorcycle?)*
>
> **More clear:** The motorcycle got a flat tire while **it** was being chased by the car.

PRACTICE 1.9

> **DIRECTIONS:** Rewrite the following sentences and make the confusing pronouns refer to the nouns in bold print. You may use two sentences if necessary.
>
> 1.   The car had a dog in the **seat.** It was brown. *(**It** is the confusing pronoun)*
> 2.   **Officer Black** and Officer White went into his house. *(**His** is the confusing pronoun)*
> 3.   The mayor told the **chief** he no longer had a job. *(**He** is the confusing pro noun)*
> 4.   The two witnesses saw the **robbers** leave the building. Then they got into their car. *(**They** is the confusing pronoun)*

CHAPTER 2

VERBS AND AGREEMENT

PERFORMANCE OBJECTIVES – After studying this chapter, you will be able to:

➤   Identify verbs in sentences.

➤   Revise present tense and future tense construction to past tense .

➤   Identify correct irregular past tense forms of verbs.

➤   Revise third person sentence construction to first person .

➤   Identify subjects in sentences.

➤   Pair subjects which are collective nouns or indefinite pronouns with singular verbs.

➤   Pair plural pronouns with plural antecedents and singular pronouns with singular antecedents.

There are at least two major reasons to learn about verbs: (1) Later, in dealing with subject-verb agreement, you must be able to recognize verbs, and (2) the correct use of verb tenses, persons and forms causes reports to be more clear.

Verbs are words that show action or existence. There may be more than one verb in a sentence.

EXAMPLES

He **ran** from the officers. *(Shows action.)*

He **should have been arrested.** *(**Arrested** is the main verb. The other verbs are sometimes called auxiliary or helping verbs.)*

He **was** a good cop. *(Shows existence, sometimes referred to as "a state of being.")*

She **walked** and **ran** for almost three miles. *(Two main verbs.)*

PRACTICE 2.1

> **DIRECTIONS: Underline the verbs. There may be more than one verb in each sentence.**
>
> 1. He is a famous jewel thief.
>
> 2. Jimmy should have been prepared.
>
> 3. Dave pursued the getaway car.
>
> 4. I ran to the hurt victim.

Every verb has tenses that change the form of the verb. The form of the verb changes the meaning of the sentence.

EXAMPLES

> I **am writing** the report.
>
> I **wrote** the report.
>
> I **will write** the report.
>
> I **have written** the report.
>
> I **had written** the report.
>
> I **will have written** one hundred reports by the end of the month.

Public safety reports are generally written **after** events occur. It is, therefore, most accurate to write reports in the past tense. Weeks, months, sometimes years after you write your report, you may have to testify. You will probably refresh your memory of events from your report. You will testify in the past tense. You no longer know if the suspect **has** a mustache (present tense). If you wrote that he has a mustache you will have to translate your report from the present tense to the past while testifying. This will be the case even if he still has a mustache because you will testify in the past tense. Haven't you got enough things on your mind when you testify?

If you wrote that he **had** a mustache (past tense) you can still accurately testify to that fact without concern for some defense attorney trying to make you look like an incompetent or a liar when he presents a clean-shaven suspect to the jury. If you wrote that he **had** a mustache that he no longer has, the jury will not think much of it. The jury might even wonder why he shaved off his mustache if the defense attorney tries to make an issue of it. Was it to change his appearance in the hopes of avoiding being identified? Are those the actions of an innocent person?

No juror expects public safety personnel to gaze into the future and predict how things will be weeks, months or years from now. Jurors **do** expect public safety personnel to accurately record events as they were when they took place or were investigated.

Write public safety reports in the past tense.

EXAMPLES

> **Bad:** The car **is** blue. *(This is **present tense** –Are you **sure** it hasn't been painted red since you wrote this?)*
>
> **Better:** The car **was** blue. *(This is **past tense**—You can write this without fear of contradiction if you were once sure of its color.)*

PRACTICE 2.2

DIRECTIONS: Change the sentences to past tense. (If you need help, dictionaries usually give the past tenses of verbs.)

1. He starts the car.

2. I will investigate the accident.

3. They run away.

4. We go to lunch.

Many verbs tell us an action was in the past simply by adding –d, -ed, or –t to the present tense.

EXAMPLES

> He died yesterday. (-d added to **die**)
>
> He was **arrested.** (-ed added to **arrest**)
>
> The card was **dealt** from the bottom of the deck. (-t added to **deal**)

Unfortunately, the past tense is often formed irregularly compared to the above examples. There are no easy rules to explain how irregular verbs change. **Use a dictionary to determine the past tenses of irregularly changing verbs.**

PRACTICE 2.3

DIRECTIONS: Underline the correct past tense form of the verbs.

1. She (drived, druv, droved, drove) the car.

2. I (brung, brought, bringt, bringed) the coffee you asked for.

3. He (broke, breaked, broked, breakt) the window.

4. The officer (finded, fund, found, findt) the knife.

Each verb has "person" which changes the form of the verb.

EXAMPLES

I **run** daily. *(First person, singular.)*

You **run** daily. *(Second person, singular.)*

He **runs** daily. *(Third person, singular.)*

We **run** daily. *(First person, plural.)*

They **run** daily. *(Third person, plural.)*

Report writing should be similar to speaking. When speaking to a colleague would you say *this person* or *Officer Smith* or *the undersigned* (all third person) when referring to yourself? Are you going to testify that way? Why not write the same way you speak (and testify)? **The person writing the reports should write in the first person.** This means *only the writers* will use the pronouns *I, me, my* and *mine* when referring to things that they do, things that are done to them or their possessions.

EXAMPLES

I hit Brown. *(First person.)*

Brown hit **me.** *(First person.)*

The flashlight was **mine.** *(First person.)*

PRACTICE 2.4

DIRECTIONS: Change the sentences to first person.

1. This writer arrested Harrington.

2. This undersigned officer pursued the red Honda.

3. The deputy (you) saw the crime occur.

4. McKenna (the writing officer) wrote the report.

If **every** party in a report (officer, suspect, victim, witnesses) used the first person it would be confusing and unnatural. The pronoun "I" used by more than one person in a story renders the story meaningless. (Unless used in a direct quote. That will be dealt with later.) **You** are telling the story of **your** investigation, **your** actions or what **you** saw. How do **you** naturally speak of others when telling a story?

When persons who are writing reports are giving the statements of suspects, victims or witnesses (other than themselves) the *third* person should be used.

EXAMPLES

Green saw Jones hit Brown. *(The writer is writing about three other people.)*

White handcuffed Green. *(White is another officer. He is **not** the officer writing the report.)*

Black said the flashlight was his.

Writing in the past tense has an added bonus. The first person, past tense and third person, past tense verbs are identical. This is true for almost all English verbs — even irregularly changing verbs — and even in their plural forms.

EXAMPLES

I **arrested** Brown. *(First person, singular, past tense.)*

We **arrested** Brown. *(First person, plural, past tense.)*

He **arrested** Brown. *(Third person, singular, past tense.)*

They **arrested** Brown. *(Third person, plural, past tense.)*

As with most rules, there is an exception. The verb *to be* is irregular in the past tense.

EXAMPLES

I **was** nervous about testifying. *(First person, singular, past tense.)*

We **were** unhappy with the jury's verdict. *(First person, plural, past tense.)*

He **was** an experienced thief. *(Third person, singular, past tense.)*

They **were** used to working together. *(Third person, plural, past tense.)*

A sentence has a minimum of two parts. One part of a sentence is the subject, the topic of the sentence. **Subjects consist of nouns or pronouns which tell us who or what did things or had things done to them and their adjectives.**

EXAMPLES

The officers began their shift at 0730 hours. *(**The officers** is the subject. It tells who did what.)*

The car was wrecked. *(**The car** is the subject. It tells what had something done to it.)*

PRACTICE 2.5

DIRECTIONS: In the following sentences identify the subjects by underlining them.

1. Their uniforms are blue.

2. Detectives are usually experienced patrol officers.

3. The burglars specialized in doctors' offices.

4. My arm is still sore.

The subject is usually the first part of a sentence but this is not always true.

EXAMPLES

Is **your partner** sick today?

There were **three deputies** surrounding the house.

PRACTICE 2.6

DIRECTIONS: In each sentence underline the subject.

1. Are there two motorcycle officers working today?

2. Into the room burst the suspect.

3. Where are Officers Smith and Jones?

4. From out of the clouds came the helicopter.

If the subject is singular, the verb in that sentence (which tells what was being done to or by the subject) must also be singular. If the subject is plural, the verb must also be plural.

EXAMPLES

Wrong: He were drunk. *(The plural verb **were** does **not** belong with the singular subject **he**.)*

Correct: He was drunk. *(**He** is the singular subject. **Was** is the singular, past tense verb.)*

Wrong: They was drunk. *(A plural subject does **not** belong with a singular verb.)*

Correct: They were drunk. *(**They** and **were** are the plural subject and verb.)*

PRACTICE 2.7

DIRECTIONS: In each of the following sentences underline the subject. Determine if it is singular or plural. Then underline the correct verb form.

1. He (was, were) in charge of the narcotics raid.

2. I (was, were) frightened.

3. We (was, were) late.

4. They (was, were) in trouble.

Do not be fooled by other nouns or pronouns in a sentence. Identify the subject. It alone controls the verb form.

EXAMPLES

Wrong: The chief, as well as his captains, were present. *(What's the subject? Is it singular or plural?)*

Correct: The chief, as well as his captains, **was** present. *(**The chief** not **his captains** is the singular subject requiring the singular verb **was**.)*

Correct: The chief and his captains were present. *(This sentence has a plural subject. **The chief and his captains** is the plural subject in this sentence, so the plural verb **were** is appropriate.)*

Collective nouns are always singular. If a collective noun is the subject of a sentence, the verb in that sentence must be singular.

EXAMPLE

> The crowd of rioters was angry. (***Crowd*** *is a collective noun requiring the use of the singular verb* ***was.****)*

> The jury was undecided. (***Jury*** *is a collective noun requiring the use of the singular verb* ***was.****)*

Indefinite pronouns are always singular. If an indefinite pronoun is the subject of a sentence, the verb in that sentence must be singular.

EXAMPLE

> **Correct:** Everyone was happy. (***Everyone*** *is an indefinite pronoun requiring the use of the singular verb* ***was.****)*

PRACTICE 2.8

DIRECTIONS: In each of the following sentences underline the correct verb form.

1. The lieutenant, followed by his sergeants, (was, were) in the parade.

2. Everybody (was, were) working hard.

3. The mob of looters (was, were) setting stores on fire.

4. The parked cars and a motorcycle (was, were) involved in the accident.

Because pronouns substitute for nouns they must agree in number with the nouns they replace.

EXAMPLES

> **Wrong:** Officers should use the pistol range only when he or she is supervised. (***Officers*** *is plural,* ***he*** *or* ***she*** *is singular because of the word* ***or*** *— one* ***or*** *the other — not both)*

> **Correct: Officers** should use the pistol range only when **they** are supervised.

>   OR

> **Correct: An officer** should use the pistol range only when **he** (or she) is supervised.

PRACTICE 2.9

DIRECTIONS: Underline the correct pronoun in each sentence.

1. Officers must remember to turn off (his or her, their) radios before entering the building.

2. An officer never forgets (their, his) first arrest.

CHAPTER 3

MODIFIERS AND SENTENCE STRUCTURE

PERFORMANCE OBJECTIVES – After studying this chapter, you will be able to:

➤ Identify adjectives in sentences.

➤ Identify adverbs in sentences.

➤ Correctly choose between adverbs and adjectives as modifiers in sentences.

➤ Choose the correct degree of comparison in sentences.

➤ Rewrite sentences containing confusing modifiers to avoid confusion.

➤ Revise sentence fragments into correct, clear and complete sentences.

➤ Revise run-on sentences into correct, clear and complete sentences.

➤ Revise comma splices into correct, clear and complete sentences.

Adjectives are words used to alter, give additional meaning to or modify nouns and pronouns.

EXAMPLE

> He wore a green shirt. (***Green*** *gives additional meaning to* ***shirt****, a noun.)*

A, an and *the* are always adjectives.

PRACTICE 3.1

DIRECTIONS: Underline the adjectives. There may be more than one adjective in each sentence.

1. The victim was pretty.
2. The two burglars were young.
3. The youngest suspect wore purple shoes.
4. The best shooter in the group was the lieutenant.

If you can easily fit a word into the phrase: He/it was very _____, it is probably an adjective. Some adjectives (such as **a, an** and **the**) will not fit into the blank. But every word that **will** fit into the blank and make sense is an adjective. When in doubt, use a dictionary.

Dictionaries usually tell if words are adjectives. Be careful though. Some words can be different things depending upon their use. **Car** is usually a noun, but in the phrase **car door**, *car* is an adjective because it gives additional meaning to the word *door*. When using a dictionary to determine if a word is an adjective (or any other part of speech) check the usage as well.

Adverbs are words used to alter, give additional meaning to or modify verbs, adjectives and other adverbs.

EXAMPLES

He ran **quickly**. (**quickly** gives additional meaning to ran, a verb.)

She was **very** pretty. (**very** gives additional meaning to pretty, an adjective.)

He ran **very** quickly. (here, **very** gives additional meaning to quickly, an adverb.)

PRACTICE 3.2

DIRECTIONS: Underline the adverbs. There may be more than one adverb in each sentence.

1. He did his work efficiently.

2. She was arrested twice for drunk driving.

3. The very young suspect wore brightly colored shoes.

4. I will gladly never do it again.

Most words ending in –ly are adverbs. *Not, never* and *very* are always adverbs. Adverbs can also be defined as words that give information on how, when and how often.

EXAMPLES

He did **poorly** on the test. *(**Poorly** tells how.)*

I like to run **early** in the morning. *(**Early** tells when.)*

I go to the shooting range **daily**. *(**Daily** tells how often.)*

When deciding whether to use an adjective or an adverb, find the word being modified. If the word being modified is a noun or pronoun, use an adjective. If the word being modified is a verb, adjective or adverb, use an adverb.

EXAMPLES

Wrong: He ran fast. *(The word being modified is **ran**. **Ran** is a verb. **Fast** is an adjective. An adjective cannot modify a verb.)*

Wrong: He ran quick. (**Quick** *is also an adjective.)*

Correct: He ran quickly. *(**Quickly** is an adverb. It can correctly be used to modify the verb **ran**.)*

PRACTICE 3.3

DIRECTIONS: Underline the correct modifier in each sentence.

1. He ate (fast, quick, quickly).

2. The chemicals smelled (awful, awfully).

3. The (heavily, heavy) armed suspects resisted arrest.

4. His mood changed (suddenly, sudden).

Both adjectives and adverbs have degrees of comparison. The first degree shows no comparison. The second degree shows comparison between two objects or qualities. The third degree shows comparison between three or more objects or qualities.

EXAMPLES

First degree of comparison: It was **small**. *(**Small** is an adjective showing no comparison)*

Second degree of comparison: It was the **smaller** one. *(**Smaller** shows comparison of two objects.)*

Third degree of comparison: It was the **smallest** one. *(**Smallest** shows comparison of three or more.)*

Some degrees of comparison change irregularly.

It was **bad**. *(**Bad** is an adverb showing no comparison.)*

It was **worse** than yesterday. *(**Worse** involves comparison of two qualities.)*

It was the **worst** of all. *(**Worst** involves comparison of three or more.)*

OR

He ran **quickly**. *(**Quickly** is an adverb showing no comparison.)*

Mary ran **more quickly** than Susan. *(Comparison of two qualities.)*

Of all those who raced, Linda ran **most quickly**. *(Comparison of three or more.)*

A good dictionary will give irregularly changing degrees of comparison. Before buying a dictionary, look up the word *bad*. If it doesn't tell you the second degree of comparison is *worse*, buy a different dictionary.

Comparatives are meaningless unless the basis for comparison is given. *Do not use comparatives if more specific information is available.*

EXAMPLES

Bad: The suspect was **tall.** *(Compared to whom? A professional basketball player? A dwarf? This is useless information.)*

Better: The suspect was **taller** than I am. *(Comparison to a known object or quality. This is meaningless unless you state your height too.)*

Best: The suspect was six feet tall. *(This is specific information requiring no comparison.)*

PRACTICE 3.4

DIRECTIONS: Underline the correct degree of comparison. You may use a dictionary.

1. She is the (intelligentest, more intelligent, most intelligent) person on the police department.

2. Of the two of them, I think Joe is (taller, more tall, more taller, tallest).

3. Officer Kearns does his work (efficienter, more efficiently, more efficienter) than Officer Herbert.

4. Compared to Pat and Dave, he reloads his pistol (quickest, most quickly, more quickly).

Modifiers need to be connected with the words they are modifying. Modifiers that are not logically connected to the words they are modifying are called dangling, squinting or misplaced modifiers. All are confusing. Regardless of the type of modifier problem, the solution is the same. **Place modifiers in sentences so they refer to only one person or thing or action.**

EXAMPLES

Confusing: I found a stain on a jacket that was red. *(Which was red? The stain? The jacket?)*

Better: I found a red stain on a jacket.

OR

Better: I found a stain on a red jacket. *(Placing the adjective **red** next to the noun it is intended to modify — **jacket** —eliminates confusion.)*

Confusing: Drinking coffee often keeps him awake. *(Placing **often** between **drinking coffee** and **keeps him awake** causes confusion. Is he kept awake often when he drinks coffee or is he kept awake only when he drinks coffee often?)*

Better: He is often kept awake by drinking coffee.

OR

Better: If he drinks coffee often, it keeps him awake.

PRACTICE 3.5

DIRECTIONS: Rewrite these sentences to avoid confusion.

1. He saw the bank rounding the corner. *(Did the bank round a corner?)*

2. Looking again, the knife seemed small. *(Did the knife look again?)*

3. Agent Tyndale found marijuana outside the car wrapped in paper. *(Was the car wrapped in paper?)*

4. He said he would paint the house last night. *(Was he really planning to paint at night?)*

    Public safety reports should be written using complete sentences. We generally speak in sentences. It makes good sense to write as we speak. Sentences have two major components. We already have dealt with both components, subjects and verbs. A sentence must have at least a subject and a verb, but every group of words containing a subject and a verb is not a sentence. **Sentences must have subjects _and_ verbs _and_ convey complete thoughts. Sentence fragments are groups of words that begin with capital letters and end with periods but are not sentences.**

EXAMPLES

Wrong: Went to the crime scene. *(This is a fragment. There is no subject.)*

Wrong: The agent in charge of the case. *(This is a fragment. There is no verb.)*

Wrong: Until he caught the suspect. *(This fragment has a subject and a verb but does not convey a complete thought.)*

Correct: Halt! *(This **is** a sentence. It is an exception to the rule that a sentence requires both a subject and verb. This is a command. The subject – **you** – is implied.)*

PRACTICE 3.6

DIRECTIONS: Rewrite as necessary to eliminate sentence fragments and form complete sentences. No corrections may be required.

1. The burglar broke the window. And entered the house.

2. She noticed the blue car. Weaving down the road.

3. He said he was sorry. He left the area.

4. The victim was afraid to testify. After she was threatened.

Run-on sentences contain what should be two or more sentences in one overly-long sentence. The separate sentences are usually joined by a connecting word such as **and** or **but**. When testifying, you should only convey one thought in response to one question. Write reports in single-thought sentences to simplify testifying. What may be acceptable, multiple-thought sentences for essay or fiction writing may be considered run-on sentences in report writing.

EXAMPLES

Bad: Fingerprints from the crime scene were found by Officer Leon and they were compared with those of the suspect. (If you can eliminate the connecting word — **and** in this case — and have two or more complete sentences, then the original sentence is a run-on sentence for report writing purposes.)

Placing a comma before **and** in the above example would technically avoid the label of a run-on sentence in an essay or work of fiction. In report writing, however, it is still best to use shorter, single-thought sentences rather than longer ones. In other words, leave out the comma *and* the word **and**. Create separate sentences whenever you can. Don't worry about your report sounding "choppy". Reports are not meant to be works of fiction. Ease of reading is less important than clarity of meaning.

Better: Fingerprints from the crime scene were found by Officer Leon.

They were compared with those of the suspect.

PRACTICE 3.7

DIRECTIONS: Rewrite the sentences if they are run-on sentences.

1. The pawnbroker saw the suspects and became suspicious and phoned the police.

2. Dave shot his pistol and cleaned it.

3. The burglar was finally booked and I went home to bed.

4. The suspect appeared in court and he acted nervously.

A comma splice occurs when a writer incorrectly joins two complete sentences with a comma and no connecting word such as *and* or *but*. Even essay and fiction writers cannot argue about this rule.

EXAMPLES

Wrong: The defendant rose from his seat, he charged at the judge. *(Two complete sentences incorrectly joined with a comma.)*

Correct: The defendant rose from his seat. He charged at the judge.

PRACTICE 3.8

DIRECTIONS: Rewrite the sentences as necessary to eliminate comma splices.

1. He left his fingerprints at the scene, I found several of them.

2. Having much work to do, he arrived early.

3. The burglars entered the building, they opened every office door.

4. If you see George before I do, say hello for me.

CHAPTER 4

PUNCTUATION

PERFORMANCE OBJECTIVES – After studying this chapter, you will be able to:

➤   State the importance of correct punctuation in public safety reports.

➤   Correctly place commas in sentences.

➤   Correctly remove unnecessary commas from sentences.

➤   Correctly place apostrophes in sentences.

➤   Use possessive pronouns without apostrophes in sentences.

➤   Correctly remove unnecessary apostrophes from sentences.

➤   Form possessives from singular and plural nouns.

➤   Correctly use parentheses, brackets, dashes, hyphens, colons, semicolons, quotation marks, underlining and italics.

Why is punctuation important in public safety reports? **Poorly punctuated reports can be confusing or even misleading.**

EXAMPLES

> The suspect's car was blue-green and white. *(This two-color car was a sort of turquoise and white.)*
>
> The suspect's car was blue/green and white. *(This three-color car was blue **over** green and white.)*
>
> The suspect's car was blue, green and white. *(This three-color car was blue, green **and** white.)*

The only differences in describing the cars above are punctuation differences. Incorrectly punctuated descriptions of these cars could cause crooks to go free and officers to be sued for false arrest!

Commas are used where the writer wants the reader to pause briefly while reading a sentence or because the meaning will be unclear without the commas.

EXAMPLES

The officers, while searching the building, found dynamite. *(Can you hear the pauses when you read this?)*

After the suspect shot John, Smith ran. *(Contrast this sentence with the next example.)*

After the suspect shot, John Smith ran. *(The comma completely changes the meaning of this example when compared to the example above.)*

PRACTICE 4.1

DIRECTIONS: Place commas where needed. Several or no commas may be needed in each sentence.

1. Did you last arrest Smith in March or was it during April?

2. Kathy a five year veteran was awarded a lifesaving medal.

3. Patrick you have done a fine job.

4. After the shooting all the people were interviewed.

A comma is also used to separate items in a series, address or date.

EXAMPLES

The colors of our flag are red, white, and blue. *(Separates items in a series. The last comma—the one just before **and**—is optional.)*

He lived at 5093 Hawley Blvd., San Diego, California. *(Separates items in an address.)*

It occurred on May 13, 1936. *(Separates items in a date.)*

PRACTICE 4.2

DIRECTIONS: Add commas where needed. Several or no commas may be needed in each sentence.

1. He lived at 1234 D E. Fourth Boulevard California.

2. The date was January 181949.

3. The stolen sweater was blue red yellow and green.

4. He was charged with theft and trespassing.

PRACTICE 4.3

DIRECTIONS: Eliminate unnecessary commas. There may be several or no unnecessary commas in each sentence.

1. He was a fine, officer.

2. She worked, and worked, on that case.

3. Detective Hoffman got angry, and broke his pencil.

4. The instructor, a hard-working individual, was intelligent, honest, well-spoken and handsome.

Apostrophes are used to show that letters (or numbers) have been left out.

EXAMPLES

You're doing a fine job. *(The apostrophe shows there are letters missing in **you are**.)*

PRACTICE 4.4

DIRECTIONS: Add apostrophes as necessary. Several or no apostrophes may be needed in each sentence.

1. Theyre having fun in their boat over there.

2. He went to the Sea n Ski Sport Shop.

3. Were going to Ricks house for the Class of 82 reunion.

4. Havent you got anything better to do at ten oclock?

Apostrophes are used to show possession.

EXAMPLE

That flashlight is Paula's. *(The apostrophe in **Paula's** shows possession)*

Possessive pronouns (such as his, hers, ours, yours, theirs and its) do not need apostrophes.

PRACTICE 4.5

DIRECTIONS: Add apostrophes where needed. There may be several or no apostrophes needed in each sentence.

1. Its hot here and I miss San Diegos cool ocean breezes.

2. There are five batteries in this flashlight.

3. Their cars are blue, ours are white.

4. Its coat is shaggy and its ugly.

To make most nouns plural and possessive add –s' to those nouns.

EXAMPLES

The boy**s'** locker room is always cleaner than the girls**'**.

The car**s'** interiors are brown. *(Referring to the interiors of two or more cars.)*

To form a possessive for a singular or plural noun ending in –s (or an "s" sound) just add the apostrophe.

EXAMPLES

It was Dennis' jacket. *(Plural possessive of a singular noun ending in –s.)*

I took the two waitress' statements. *(Plural possessive of a plural noun ending in –s.)*

PRACTICE 4.6

DIRECTIONS: Place apostrophes where needed. There may be several or no apostrophes needed in each sentence.

1. It was Willis car.

2. The two repossessors papers were in order.

3. The three officers pistols were inspected.

4. The duchess limousine was black.

Apostrophes are not used to form plurals except for plurals of letters and figures.

EXAMPLES

Correct: I got straight A's on my report card. *(Plural of a letter, number or* figure.)

Wrong: These were excellent grade's. *(Do not use apostrophes to form plurals of nouns.)*

PRACTICE 4.7

DIRECTIONS: Add or eliminate apostrophes as necessary. There may be several or no apostrophe corrections in each sentence.

1. The hay bale's were not theirs.

2. There's no difference between Shelly's and Ann's pistol's.

3. The criminals faces were not visible to the witness's.

4. Your brothers sister had several ?s on her test paper.

Parentheses are used to enclose supplementary information. **Parentheses can be replaced by commas where the supplementary information they enclose is essential. Parentheses can be left out entirely where the supplementary information is not essential. Since non-essential information should be left out of reports, don't use parentheses to enclose supplementary information in reports.**

EXAMPLES

Bad: Officer Kopkowski (the arresting officer) gave the suspect first aid. *(If the information is essential, use commas.)*

Better: Officer Kopkowski, the arresting officer, gave the suspect first aid. (Essential supplementary information is set off by commas.)

> OR

Better: Officer Kopkowski gave the suspect first aid. *(If the supplementary information is not essential, leave it out completely.)*

Parentheses may be used to enclose numbers which are not mere repeating of spelled-out numbers.

EXAMPLE

The robber took three things: (1) a purse, (2) a wallet and (3) a watch.

Using parentheses to repeat a spelled-out number with a number enclosed in parentheses adds nothing but length to your report.

EXAMPLE

Wrong: The robber took three (3) things. *(Was there any confusion requiring the number in parentheses? No. The parentheses were not needed here.)*

Brackets are properly used to set off the writer's comments inside a quote of another writer being quoted.

EXAMPLE

The witness said, "The tall suspect [Brown] took my purse." *(Here the writer— not the witness — used the suspect's name.)*

If you wrote the above example, might a juror think the witness knew the suspect's name? Might a defense attorney suggest to the jury that you were deliberately trying to mislead the jury? **Because most people do not understand the rules for using brackets, don't use them in public safety reports.**

PRACTICE 4.8

DIRECTIONS: Rewrite the sentences as necessary to correctly use parentheses and brackets.

1. The suspect said his [*Miranda*] rights had been violated.

2. The victim (a prostitute) was found in a ditch.

3. I found twelve (12) balloons of heroin in the suspect's pockets.

4. Brown was read his rights (by Officer Jones) before he was questioned.

Dashes are not the same as hyphens and do not serve the same purposes in sentences. The only visual difference between a dash and a hyphen is the length of the dash. It's longer than a hyphen. Dashes, like parentheses, can usually be replaced with commas in public safety reports. Similarly, if the information set off by dashes is nonessential to the public safety report, leave it out.

EXAMPLES

Bad: Dashes — like parentheses — can usually be replaced with commas.

Bad: Dashes (like parentheses) can usually be replaced with commas.

Better: Dashes, like parentheses, can usually be replaced with commas.

OR

Better: Dashes can usually be replaced with commas.

Hyphens are best used (1) to spell out compound numbers between twenty and one hundred, (2) to avoid confusion, (3) with some prefixes and suffixes and (4) in place of the word "to".

EXAMPLES

He had twenty-three prior moving violations. *(Compound number.)*

He had to re-press the suit. *(The hyphen here is used to avoid confusion—compare to **repress the suit**.)*

His ex-wife had possession of their children. *(Hyphen after the prefix **ex**.)*

He received a prison sentence of 2-5 years. *(Use of a hyphen in place of the word **to**.)*

A hyphen is used in place of the word *to*, not *through*. If you write something occurred March 3-March 6, you're saying it happened up to March 6, but not *including* March 6. If you wish to include March 6 in this example, write the word *through* or *thru* instead of using a hyphen to avoid confusion.

Hyphens are also used to separate syllables of words when only part of a word will fit on a line of writing. Many people do not know how to divide words into syllables for this purpose. If you're writing reports by hand, it is easiest to put entire words on lines to avoid confusion. If you're using a word processor, the program may divide words at their syllables automatically or only after you give a command to do so.

PRACTICE 4.9

DIRECTIONS: Rewrite the sentences as necessary to correctly use dashes and hyphens.

1. The suspect — after seeing the evidence — confessed.

2. There were twenty one ounce vials.

3. My sergeant — he plays a mean game of racquetball — headed up the investigation.

4. I will be on vacation August 8-22.

Colons have only one legitimate use in public safety reports. **Colons are used to introduce lists.**

EXAMPLE

The robber took three things: (1) a purse, (2) a wallet and (3) a watch.

Colons have other uses generally **not** found in public safety report writing. These include the use of colons after salutations in business letters and the use of colons separating hours from minutes in twelve-hour time. Twelve-hour time requires the writer to include am or pm information. **Military (or 24-hour) time contains no colons and eliminates possible am or pm confusion.**

EXAMPLES

Bad: The crime took place at **1:32 am**. *(If the writer forgot to include am, would you know when this occurred?)*

Better: The crime took place at **0132 hours**. *(There is no way to confuse this with 1:32 pm.)*

OR

Bad: The crime took place at **1:32 pm.**

Better: The crime took place at **1332 hours**. (After 1200 hours, simply continue the numerical sequence.)

Semicolons only have two legitimate functions. They are used in series of things containing commas, and they are used to join two simple sentences. The first function is unlikely to occur in public safety reports and the second does nothing but attempt to legitimatize run-on sentences. Neither of these semicolon functions is appropriate for public safety reports.

EXAMPLES

B.A., English, San Diego State College; M.A., Education, San Diego State University *(The semicolon separates items in a series containing commas.)*

The defendant was read his *Miranda* rights; he decided not to talk. *(Two simple sentences are joined by a semicolon. It would be better to make two separate sentences.)*

Since neither of the legitimate functions of semicolons above is likely to arise in public safety reports, simply do not use semicolons in public safety reports.

PRACTICE 4.10

DIRECTIONS: Rewrite the sentences as necessary correctly using colons and semicolons.

1. Dorie said: "I'm not talking without my lawyer."

2. The victim saw the suspect entering a window; he yelled at him.

3. There were five pieces of evidence: a photograph, a shirt, a wallet, a knife and a shoe.

4. The traffic officer looked at the accident scene; he saw a skid mark he had not seen before.

Most people understand that words enclosed in quotation marks are a person's exact words. **Use quotation marks only to enclose exactly what a person said.**

EXAMPLES

> **Correct:** Smith said, "I'll talk to you without my lawyer being here."
> *(Exact quote)*
>
> **Wrong:** Smith said something like, "It's OK if we talk without a lawyer."
> *(This is a confusing use of quotation marks. Did he say this or something like this?)*

The overuse of quotation marks can cause problems for public safety personnel. Suppose two officers extensively quote a suspect while they testify. What will happen if they remember the quotes differently? Might some defense attorney try to use that to show the officers are incompetent? Might the defense attorney suggest to the jury that one of the officers must be lying? If there are very few quotes, the chances of all parties remembering the quotes similarly improve.

Use quotation marks to exactly quote a person only (1) when helping to prove the elements of the crime, (2) when necessarily using slang or (3) when quoting a suspect's profanity.

EXAMPLES

> **Bad:** The victim said, "I called the police." *(This quote is not needed.)*
>
> **Better:** The victim said she called the police. *(This is the correct way to deal with unnecessary quoted—don't use them.)*
>
> **Correct:** Smith said he "wiped out" Brown. *(This tells the reader that the slang phrase **wiped out** is Smith's, not yours.)*
>
> **Correct:** Smith said, "Fuck that breath test shit." *(Though this does not prove guilt, profanity is very damaging when presented to a jury.)*

The rules for underlining and italics are the same. When word processing, use italics if you can. When writing by hand or typing, use underlining for exactly the same reasons as you would use italics. Italics and underlining are only likely to be needed in public safety reports when giving the names of legal cases.

EXAMPLES

Correct: <u>Mapp</u> v. <u>Ohio</u> was a very important case. *(Underline when writing by hand or otherwise not able to italicize case names.)*

Correct: *Mapp* v. *Ohio* was a very important case. *(Italicize case names when you can, underline when you cannot italicize.)*

Correct: I read the *Miranda* rights to him. *(This shortened case name requires the same treatment as the entire case name.)*

PRACTICE 4.11

DIRECTIONS: Rewrite the sentences as necessary to correctly use quotation marks, underlining and italics.

1. Robinson said, "I hope you catch those guys."

2. I searched the car within the guidelines established in the case of U.S. v. Ross.

3. Rick said he only roughed her up.

4. Jones said, "You found my marijuana."

CHAPTER 5

CAPITALIZATION, ABBREVIATIONS AND SPELLING

PERFORMANCE OBJECTIVES – After studying this chapter, you will be able to:

➤ Correctly use standard abbreviations and capitalization.

➤ Correctly spell words most often misspelled in public safety reports.

Problems in capitalization are easily cured. **USE NOTHING BUT CAPITAL LETTERS IN HANDWRITTEN REPORTS**. A lower case hand-printed *d* looks very much like a lower case hand-printed *a*. In many words the correct letter can be figured out because only one or the other will make any sense. But in a serial number, license number or unusual name there must be no doubt as to what you intend to write. No two capital letters look enough alike to allow confusion. Even when typing or word processing your reports you will make them easier to read and avoid wrestling with capitalization rules if you simply use all capital letters.

In most jurisdictions, public safety reports are potential evidence. Jurors may read the reports while deliberating on a verdict and you will not be there to explain the abbreviations to them. **Do not use abbreviations in public safety reports that can be confusing to people who are totally unfamiliar with public safety work. When in doubt, spell it out.**

EXAMPLES

Bad: He was **O.D.** *(Was he overdosed or off-duty?)*

Bad: Evidence: **DNA** *(Does not apply or deoxyribonucleic acid?)*

Better: Dr. Rick did the examination of the specimen. *(This is acceptable although it includes people with Ph.D.'s, dentists and veterinarians.)*

Better: Agent James was from the **FBI.** *(No juror would have trouble with this.)*

PRACTICE 5.1

DIRECTIONS: Rewrite as necessary to properly use abbreviations and capitalization.

1. The suspect was GOA.

2. I gave the evidence to lt. johnson of the BPD.

3. Henry st. intersects bowling dr.

4. He was assigned to CSU.

Would you let a doctor operate on you if you knew he could not spell *surgeon*? Why not? **Poor spelling is a quick and sure way to be unimpressive**. Worse, it can lead to misunderstandings about your case and laughter by the jury at your expense.

EXAMPLE

Defense attorney: *Officer, is this your report?*

Officer: *Yes, it is.*

Defense attorney: *How does a person rape cocaine?*

Officer: *I don't understand the question.*

Defense attorney: *It says here in your report "the cocaine was raped in paper."*

(Chuckles from some members of the jury)

Defense attorney: *Was that a mistake?*

Officer: *I guess it was.*

Defense attorney: *Ladies and gentlemen of the jury, we have here an officer who, by his own admission, makes mistakes in public safety reports. I submit to you that an officer who makes one mistake might well make others. Maybe he made a mistake when he wrote in his report that he saw my client commit the crime.*

I remind you of your oaths as jurors that, if there is a reasonable doubt in your minds as to the guilt or innocence of my client, you must find him not guilty.

English is composed of words from several different languages including German, French, Celtic, Latin and Greek. Unlike most of those languages in their pure form, English often is **not** spelled as it sounds. Therefore you cannot rely on how an English word sounds to determine its spelling.

EXAMPLES

> **Question:** What does **ghoti** spell? (Hint: Use the **gh** sound from cou**gh**, the **o** sound from w**o**men and the **ti** sound from par**ti**al.)
>
> **Answer: Ghoti** spells **fish.**
>
> **Question:** In English words, how many different ways are there to pronounce the combination of letters made up by **ough?**
>
> **Answer**: Th**ough**t, thr**ough**, th**ough**, t**ough**, b**ough** *(One combination of letters can have five pronunciations.)*

One way of easing the spelling burden is through your choice of words.

EXAMPLES

> Question: How do you spell **penitentiary**?
>
> **Answer: P-R-I-S-O-N**
>
> Question: How do you spell **contusion**?
>
> Answer: **B-R-U-I-S-E**

If you can use a common word that means the same thing as a less common word, use the common word. If you must use a word that you can't spell, use a dictionary to check your spelling.

Memorizing rules of English spelling takes longer than memorizing spellings of frequently misspelled words themselves. In California, the Commission on Peace Officer Standards and Training (POST) requires public safety recruits to demonstrate the ability to spell job-related words. Failure to do so could result in dismissal from the public safety academy.

A very long list of such words is here provided. It begins on the following page. These words were obtained directly from non-copyrighted material of the California Commission of Peace Officer Standards and Training for use in their basic public safety academy course.

Frankly, **there are many words here for which shorter and more commonly used words should be used.** The word *assaulted*, for instance, is longer, less often used, more difficult to spell and not nearly as informative as the word *kicked*. These longer, less common words are included in case some misguided instructor insists on making you learn the spellings of words that he should be hoping you will never use.

You may already know how to spell many of these words. Go over them with a friend. Write down those you cannot correctly spell on the first try. Memorize the spellings of ten of these words a day.

FREQUENTLY MISSPELLED WORDS
NOTE: The words are in alphabetical order if you read <u>across</u> the page.

A –

ABANDON	ABANDONED	ABBREVIATE	ABDUCTION
ABOARD	ABORTION	ABOVE	ABRASION
ABSENCE	ABSORB	ABSTRACT	ABSURD
ABUTMENT	ACCELERATE	ACCEPT	ACCESS
ACCESSIBLE	ACCESSORIES	ACCESSORY	ACCIDENT
ACCIDENTAL	ACCIDENTALLY	ACCOMMODATE	ACCOMPANIED
ACCOMPLICE	ACCOUNT	ACCUMULATE	ACCURATE
ACCUSATION	ACCUSATORY	ACCUSED	ACCUSTOM
ACCUSTOMED	ACETYLENE	ACHE	ACHIEVEMENT
ACKNOWLEDGING	ACKNOWLEDGEMENT	ACOUSTIC	ACQUAINT
ACQUAINTANCE	ACQUAINTED	ACQUIRED	ACQUITTED
ACROSS	ACTIVIST	ADAPTER	ADDICTED
ADDICTION	ADDITIONAL	ADDRESS	ADEQUATE
ADHERENCE	ADJOURN	ADJUST	ADJUSTABLE
ADJUSTER	ADMINISTER	ADMINISTRATION	ADMISSIBLE
ADMISSION	ADMITTED	ADMONISH	ADMONITION
ADOLESCENT	ADULTERY	ADVANTAGEOUS	ADVERTISEMENT
ADVICE	ADVISE	AFFECT	AFFIRMATIVE
AFRAID	AFFIDAVIT	AGAIN	AGGRAVATE
AGGRAVATED	AGGRESSIVE	AGGRESSOR	AGITATOR
AGONIZING	AGRICULTURE	AIRPLANE	AISLE
ALCOHOL	ALIAS	ALIBI	ALIEN
ALIMONY	ALLEGATION	ALLEGE	ALLEGED
ALLEY	ALLOTMENT	ALL RIGHT	ALMOST
ALTERCATION	ALTERNATE	ALTERNATIVE	ALTHOUGH
ALTOGETHER	ALWAYS	AMATEUR	AMBITIOUS
AMBULANCE	AMENDMENT	AMMETER	AMMUNITION
AMNESIA	AMONG	AMOUNT	AMPHETAMINE
AMPUTATION	AMUSEMENT	ANALYSIS	ANALYZE
ANALYZED	ANNIVERSARY	ANNOUNCE	ANNOYANCE
ANNUAL	ANNULMENT	ANONYMOUS	ANTISEPTIC
ANXIETY	ANXIOUS	APARTMENT	APOLOGIZE
APPARATUS	APPAREL	APPEAR	APPRECIATION
APPARENT	APPEAL	APPEARANCE	APPLICATION
APPREHEND	APPROPRIATE	APPROXIMATELY	AQUEDUCT
ARBITRARY			

B –

BACKWARD	BACTERIA	BAGGAGE	BAIL
BAILIFF	BALLOT	BANDAGE	BANDANNA
BARBITURATE	BARREL	BARRELED	BARRICADE
BATON	BATTERY	BAYONET	BAZAAR
BECAUSE	BEGINNING	BEHAVIOR	BELIEVE
BELLIGERENT	BENEFICIAL	BENEFIT	BENEFITED
BENZEDRINE	BEQUEATH	BETTER	BETTOR
BEVELED	BEVERAGE	BICYCLE	BIGAMY

BINOCULARS
BLOOD
BORDER
BOUQUET
BREAK
BRIBERY
BRUISE
BUOYANCE

BIZARRE
BLOWN
BOULDER
BRAKE
BREATH
BRIEF
BUILT
BUREAU

BLACKMAIL
BOISTEROUS
BOULEVARD
BRASSIERE
BREATHALYZER
BRILLIANT
BULLETIN
BURGLARY

BLEW
BOOKKEEPING
BOUNDARY
BREADTH
BREVITY
BROCHURE
BUMPER

C –

CAFETERIA
CALCULATE
CALENDAR
CANVASS
CANYON
CAPABLE
CAREFUL
CARRYING
CARTILAGE
CAUTION
CEILING
CEMETERY
CHARACTER
CHARACTERISTICS
CHAUFFEUR
CIRCUMFERENCE
CIRCUMSTANTIAL
CITABLE
COCAINE
CODEINE
COERCION
COLUMN
COMBATED
COMBUSTIBLE
COMMUNICATE
COMMUNICATIONS
COMMUNIQUÉ
COMPLEXION
COMPLIANCE
COMPULSORY
CONSCIENCE
CONSCIENTIOUS
CONSCIOUS
CONSTABLE
CONSTITUTION
CONSTRUCTION
CONVENIENCE
CONVEYOR
CONVICTION
CORPSE
CORPUS DELICTI

CALIBER
CALIPER
CAMPAIGN
CAPACITY
CAPILLARY
CAPITAL
CARTRIDGE
CASHIER
CASUAL
CENSOR
CENTER
CEREAL
CHEMICAL
CHEVROLET
CHIEF
CITATION
CITIZEN
CIVIL
COINCIDE
COINCIDENCE
COLLABORATE
COMFORTABLE
COMING
COMMENCE
COMMUNITY
COMPARISON
COMPENSATE
COMPRESS
CONCEALED
CONCUSSION
CONSCIOUSNESS
CONSECUTIVE
CONSENSUS
CONSUMMATE
CONTAGIOUS
CONTINUATION
CONVULSION
COOPERATE
COOPERATION
CORRESPONDENCE
CORROBORATE

CANAL
CANCELED
CANCELLATION
CAPITOL
CAPTAIN
CAPTURE
CASUALTIES
CASUALTY
CATALOG
CERTIFICATE
CERTIFIED
CESAREAN
CHOOSE
CHOSE
CHRYSLER
CLASSIFICATION
CLEARANCE
CLIENTELE
COLLAR
COLLEGE
COLLIDE
COMMERCIAL
COMMISSION
COMMIT
COMPENSATION
COMPETENT
COMPETITION
CONDITION
CONFESSION
CONFIDANT
CONSENT
CONSEQUENCES
CONSEQUENTLY
CONTINUE
CONTINUITY
CONTINUOUS
CORNERS
CORONER
CORPORAL
COULD
COUNCILMAN

CANDIDATE
CANISTER
CANNOT
CARBURETOR
CARDIAC
CAREER
CATASTROPHE
CATSUP
CAUCASIAN
CHAISE
CHANNELED
CHAPERON
CIGARETTE
CIRCLE
CIRCULATE
CLOTHES
CLUE
COASTAL
COLLISION
COLONEL
COLOR
COMMITMENT
COMMITTED
COMMITTEE
COMPLAINANT
COMPLAINT
COMPLETE
CONFUSED
CONGREGATE
CONNECTED
CONSISTENT
CONSPICUOUS
CONSPIRACY
CONTRABAND
CONTRIBUTING
CONTUSION
CORPORATION
COOPERATIVE
CORPS
COUNSELED
COUNSELOR

CORRECTIVE	COUGH	COUNTERFEIT	COUPON
CREDITOR	CRIMINALLY	CRUISING	COURTEOUS
CRIMINAL	CRITICISM	CRYSTALLIZED	CREDIBILITY
CRIMINALIST	CRUELTY	CURSORY	CUSTODY
CUSTOMARY	CYLINDER		

D –

DAMAGE	DANGEROUS	DAUGHTER	DAZZLING
DEADLY	DEBRIS	DEBT	DECEASED
DECEIVE	DECEIVED	DECEPTIVE	DECISION
DECOMPOSITION	DEFECATE	DEFECATED	DEFENDANT
DEFERENCE	DEFENSE	DEFENSIVE	DEFINITE
DEFINITION	DELEGATE	DELIBERATE	DELINQUENCY
DELINQUENT	DEMARCATION	DEMONSTRATE	DEMONSTRATION
DEMURRED	DENIED	DEPENDENT	DEPLOYED
DEPLOYMENT	DEPOSITION	DEPRESSANT	DEPRESSION
DESCEND	DESCENDANT	DESCRIBE	DESCRIPTION
DESECRATER	DESIGNATE	DESIGNATED	DESPERATE
DESPONDENT	DESTINATION	DETAINED	DETACHABLE
DETAILS	DETERMINE	DETERRENCE	DETERRENT
DETRIMENTAL	DEVELOP	DEVIATION	DEVICE
DEXEDRINE	DIABETES	DIAGNOSE	DIAGNOSIS
DIAGONAL	DIAGRAM	DIAGRAMED	DIAMOND
DIAPHRAGM	DIARRHEA	DICTIONARY	DIESEL
DIFFERENT	DIFFUSE	DILAPIDATED	DILATED
DINING	DIRECTION	DISAGREEABLE	DISAPPEAR
DISAPPEARANCE	DISAPPOINT	DISARRANGED	DISASTER
DISASTROUS	DISCIPLINE	DISCREET	DISCREPANCIES
DISCREPANCY	DISEASE	DISGUISE	DISHEVELED
DISK	DISLOCATION	DISMISS	DISPATCHED
DISPERSE	DISPOSITION	DISPUTE	DISSATISFIED
DISSENSION	DISSIPATION	DISTINCTION	DISTRIBUTOR
DISTRICT	DISTURBANCE	DIVERT	DIVIDE
DIVISION	DIVORCEE	DOCTOR	DOUBTFUL
DOWELED	DOWNWARD	DRUNKEN	DRUNKENNESS
DUAL	DUPLICATE	DURING	DYING

E –

EARLY	EASTWARD	EASY	ECCENTRIC
EDGEWISE	EFFECT	EFFICIENCY	EFFICIENT
EIGHT	EIGHTH	EITHER	ELECTRICITY
ELIGIBLE	ELIMINATE	EMBARRASS	EMBEZZLEMENT
EMERGENCY	EMISSIONS	EMPLOYEE	EMPLOYMENT
ENCASE	ENCLOSURE	ENFORCE	ENFORCEMENT
ENOUGH	ENTHUSIASM	ENTRANCE	ENVELOPE
ENEMY	ENVIRONMENT	EPILEPSY	EPILEPTIC
EQUAL	EQUIPMENT	EQUIPPED	EQUIVALENT
ERRATIC	ERRATICALLY	ESPECIALLY	ESSENTIAL
ETHICS	EUPHORIA	EVACUEE	EVASIVE
EVIDENCE	EVERY	EXAGGERATE	EXAMINED
EXCEEDING	EXCELLENT	EXCEPTION	EXCESSIVE

EXCITE EXCITEMENT EXCUSE EXERCISED
EXERCISED EXHAUST EXHIBIT EXHIBITION
EXHIBITOR EXISTENCE EXONERATE EXPEDITE
EXPERIENCE EXPLANATION EXPLOSION EXPOSE
EXPRESSION EXTENSION EXTINGUISH EXTORTION
EXTRADITION EXTREMELY EYEING

F –

FABRIC FACILITATE FACILITY FACSIMILE
FACTUAL FADED FAMILIAR FANTASY
FARTHER FASCINATING FATAL FATALITY
FAUCET FAVOR FEBRUARY FECAL
FECES FEDERAL FELONY FEMININE
FETAL FETUS FIBER FICTITIOUS
FIGHT FILIGREE FINALLY FINANCIAL
FISCAL FLAMMABLE FLIER FLIPPED
FLUORESCENT FOCUSED FORCIBLE FORCIBLY
FOREIGN FOREMAN FOREST FORFEIT
FORFEITURE FORGERY FORMULA FORTY
FOUND FOURTEEN FOURTH FRACTURE
FRAUDULENT FREIGHT FREQUENCY FRIEND
FRIGHTENED FUGITIVE FULFILL FUNNEL
FURNITURE FUROR FURTHER FUTILE

G –

GAIETY GAMBLING GARAGE GARBAGE
GARDENER GARROTE GASSED GAUGE
GENERALLY GENERATOR GENUINE GHETTO
GLANCING GLYCERIN GOUGE GOVERNMENT
GOVERNOR GRADUALLY GRATIFICATION GRAVELED
GREASE GRIEVANCE GUARANTEE GUARD
GUARDIAN GUERRILLA GUESSED GUEST
GUIDANCE GUILTY GUITAR GUTTURAL
GYMNASIUM GYPSY

H –

HABEAS CORPUS HABITS HABITUAL HABITUALLY
HALF HALLOWEEN HALLUCINATION HALLUCINOGEN
HANDKERCHIEF HARASS HAUGHTY HAZARD
HEADACHE HEALTHY HEAR HEARD
HEAVY HEIGHT HEMOPHILIA HEMORRHAGE
HEREDITARY HEROIN HICCUP HIDEOUS
HIJACK HINDERED HISPANIC HOLIDAY
HOMICIDE HORIZONTAL HUMANE HUMILIATE
HOMICIDE HORIZONTAL HUMANE HUMILIATE
HURRIED HURRYING HYDRAULIC HYPODERMIC

I –

IDEAL	IDENTIFIABLE	IDENTIFICATION	IDIOSYNCRASY
IGNORANCE	ILLEGAL	ILLEGITIMATE	ILLICIT
ILLITERATE	IMAGINARY	IMAGINATION	IMITATION
IMMEDIATE	IMMEDIATELY	IMMORAL	IMMUNITY
IMPANELED	IMPATIENT	IMPEDE	IMPERFECT
IMPLEMENT	IMPLICATE	IMPLIED	IMPORTANT
IMPOSE	IMPOSSIBLE	IMPOSTER	IMPOUNDED
IMPRESSION	IMPRISONMENT	INADEQUATE	INADMISSIBLE
INAUGURATE	INCARCERATION	INCENDIARY	INCESSANTLY
INCIDENT	INCIDENTALLY	INCINERATOR	INCISED
INCISION	INCITE	INCOHERENT	INCOMPETENT
INCONSISTENT	INCORRIGIBLE	INCREDIBLE	INDECENT
INDEFINITE	INDEPENDENT	INDICT	INDICTMENT
INDIFFERENT	INDIVIDUAL	INEVITABLE	INFAMOUS
INFLUENCE	INFORMANT	INFORMATION	INFRACTION
INGENIOUS	INGREDIENT	INHABITANT	INHALATION
INITIAL	INITIATE	INJECTION	INJURED
INJURY	INNOCENCE	INNOCENT	INNOCUOUS
INOCULATE	INQUIRE	INQUIRY	INQUISITIVE
INSANITY	INSCRIBE	INSCRIPTION	INSENSIBLE
INSIGHT	INSINUATE	INSTALLATION	INSTEAD
INSTINCT	INSUFFICIENT	INSURANCE	INSURE
INTELLECTUAL	INTELLIGENT	INTENDED	INTERCEDED
INTERCEPT	INTEREST	INTERIOR	INTERMITTENT
INTERN	INTERPRET	INTERROGATE	INTERROGATION
INTERRUPTED	INTERSECT	INTERSECTION	INTERSTATE
INTESTINE	INTIMIDATION	INTOXICATED	INTOXICATION
INTOXILYZER	INTOXIMETER	INVASION	INVESTIGATE
INVESTIGATION	INVOLUNTARY	IODINE	IRIDESCENT
IRRELEVANT	IRRESISTIBLE	IRRESPONSIBLE	IRREVERSIBLE
IRRIGATE	IRRITATED	IRRITATION	ISOLATE
ISSUED	ITS		

J –

JABBING	JALOPY	JEALOUS	JEOPARDIZE
JEOPARDY	JERKED	JEWELED	JEWELRY
JUDGE	JUDGMENT	JUDICIARY	JUJITSU
JURISDICTION	JUSTICE	JUSTIFIABLE	JUSTIFICATION

K –

KEROSENE	KHAKI	KIBITZER	KIDNAPPED
KILOGRAM	KNOW	KNOWLEDGE	KNUCKLES

L –

LABEL	LABORATORY	LACERATION	LANGUAGE
LARCENY	LATENT	LATER	LATTER
LAWYER	LEDGER	LEGAL	LEGALIZE
LEGALLY	LEGIBLE	LEGION	LEGISLATOR

LEGISLATOR	LEGISLATURE	LEGITIMATE	LEISURE
LENIENT	LENGTH	LENS	LESSEE
LESSOR	LEUKEMIA	LEVELED	LEWD
LIABLE	LIABILITIES	LIABILITY	LIAISON
LIBEL	LIBRARY	LICENSE	LIEN
LIEUTENANT	LIGHTNING	LIKABLE	LIKELY
LIQUEFY	LIQUID	LIQUOR	LITERATURE
LITIGATION	LITTERBUG	LIVABLE	LOCATION
LOITERING	LONELINESS	LOOSE	LOSE
LOSING	LUGGAGE	LUSTER	

M –

MACHINIST	MAGAZINE	MAGISTRATE	MAINTAIN
MAINTENANCE	MAJORITY	MALICE	MALICIOUS
MANAGEABLE	MANAGEMENT	MANEUVER	MANIFESTED
MANNEQUIN	MANSLAUGHTER	MANTEL	MANUAL
MANUFACTURER	MANUFACTURING	MANY	MARGARINE
MARGIN	MARIJUANA	MARITAL	MARRIAGE
MARSHAL	MASCULINE	MATERIAL	MATINEE
MATURITY	MAYHEM	MEAGER	MEANING
MEANT	MEASUREMENT	MEDAL	MEDIAN
MEDICAL	MEDITATE	MEMORANDUM	MEMORIAL
MEMORIZE	MENACE	MENTALLY	MERELY
METAL	MICROPHONE	MILEAGE	MILLIMETER
MINIATURE	MINIMUM	MINOR	MINORITY
MINUTE	MIRROR	MISCELLANEOUS	MISCHIEF
MISCHIEVOUS	MISCONDUCT	MISDEMEANOR	MISSPELL
MOBILE	MOCCASIN	MODEL	MODELED
MODERNIZE	MOISTURE	MOLESTED	MONETARY
MONOGRAMMED	MONOTONOUS	MORALE	MOTORCYCLE
MOUNTAINOUS	MOVABLE	MUCUS	MUFFLER
MULTIPLE	MUNICIPAL	MURDERED	MURMUR
MUSCLE	MUSEUM	MUSTACHE	

N –

NARCOTIC	NARRATIVE	NARROW	NATURAL
NECESSITY	NEGATIVE	NEGLECT	NEGLIGENCE
NEIGHBOR	NEIGHBORHOOD	NEITHER	NEPHEW
NERVOUS	NEUTRAL	NICKEL	NIECE
NIGHT	NINETY	NOISY	NORMALLY
NOTICEABLE	NOTICING	NOTIFICATION	NOTIFIED
NUISANCE	NUMEROUS		

O –

OBJECTIVELY	OBLIGATION	OBNOXIOUS	OBSCENE
OBSCENITY	OBSCURE	OBSERVATION	OBSTACLE
OBSTRUCTED	OBTAINED	OBVIOUS	OCCASION
OCCUPANT	OCCUPATION	OCCUR	OCCURRED

OCCURRENCE	OCCURS	ODOR	OFFENSE
OFFENSIVE	OFFICER	OFFICIAL	OFTEN
OMISSION	OMITTED	ONCE	ONCOMING
OPERATOR	OPINION	OPPONENT	OPPORTUNITY
OPPOSITE	OPTIMISM	ORCHESTRA	ORDINANCE
ORDINARY	ORDNANCE	ORGANIZED	ORIENTAL
ORIGINAL	OUTRAGEOUS	OVERRUN	OVERT
OXYGEN			

P –

PAINFUL	PAJAMAS	PAMPHLET	PANELED
PARAFFIN	PARAGRAPH	PARALLEL	PARAPHERNALIA
PARCEL	PAROLE	PARTIAL	PARTIALLY
PARTICULAR	PARTNER	PASSENGER	PASTIME
PATIENCE	PATROLLING	PAVEMENT	PECULIAR
PEDAL	PEDESTRIAN	PEDDLER	PENALIZE
PENALTY	PENCILED	PERFORM	PERFORMANCE
PERFORMED	PERHAPS	PERIL	PERILED
PERIMETER	PERISHABLE	PERMANENT	PERMISSIBLE
PERQUISITE	PERSECUTE	PERSEVERANCE	PERSISTENT
PERSONAL	PERSPECTIVE	PERSPIRATION	PERSUADE
PERTINENT	PERVERSION	PETITION	PHLEGM
PHYSICAL	PHYSICIAN	PICNIC	PICNICKING
PIECE	PIERCE	PLANNING	PLEA
PLEASANT	PNEUMATIC	PNEUMONIA	POISON
POISONOUS	POLICIES	PORNOGRAPHIC	PORTION
POSSESS	POSSESSION	POSSIBLE	POSSIBLY
PRACTICAL	PRACTICALLY	PRACTICE	PRECEDE
PRECEDING	PRECISE	PREDICAMENT	PREDOMINANT
PREFERABLE	PREFERENCE	PREGNANT	PREJUDICE
PRELIMINARY	PREMISES	PREPARATION	PRESCRIPTION
PRESENCE	PRESERVATION	PRESSURE	PRESUMED
PRESUMPTIVE	PRETENSE	PREVALENT	PREVENTIVE
PREVIOUSLY	PRIED	PRIMA FACIE	PRINCIPAL
PRINCIPLE	PRISONER	PROBABLE	PROBABLY
PROBATION	PROCEDURE	PROCEED	PROCEEDED
PROCESS	PROFESSION	PROFESSIONAL	PROGRAMMED
PROGRESS	PROHIBIT	PROHIBITED	PROMISSORY
PROMOTIONAL	PRONOUNCE	PRONUNCIATION	PROPELLANT
PROPERTY	PROPHECY	PROPOSITION	PROSECUTE
PROSECUTION	PROSECUTOR	PROSPECTIVE	PROSTITUTION
PSYCHOLOGICAL	PSYCHOLOGY	PUBLICITY	PULMONARY
PULSE	PUNCTURED	PUNISHABLE	PUNITIVE
PURCHASING	PURSUIT		

Q –

QUALIFICATION	QUALITY	QUANTITY	QUARANTINE
QUARREL	QUARRELED	QUERY	QUESTION
QUESTIONING	QUESTIONNAIRE	QUEUE	QUIET
QUININE	QUITE	QUOTA	QUOTED

R –

RACIAL	RACKET	RADAR	RAID
RAISE	RATIO	RATION	RATTAN
READILY	REALIZE	REALLY	REASONABLE
RECEDE	RECEIPT	RECEIVE	RECEIVING
RECIPE	RECIPIENT	RECKLESS	RECOGNIZANCE
RECOGNIZE	RECOLLECT	RECOGNIZE	RECOMMEND
RECREATION	REDUCE	REFERENCE	REFERRED
REFUSE	REFLECTOR	REFRAIN	REFUTABLE
REGISTERED	REGISTRAR	REGISTRATION	RELEASED
RELEVANT	RELIGIOUS	REINFORCE	REMEDIAL
REMEMBRANCE	REMITTANCE	RENEWAL	REPEAT
REPELLENT	REPETITION	REPOSSESSION	REPRESENTATION
REPUTATION	REQUIREMENT	RESIDENCE	RESISTANCE
RESOLUTION	RESPIRATION	RESPONSIBILITY	RESPONSIBLE
RESTAURANT	RESTRAINED	RESUSCITATION	RESUSCITATOR
REVOKED	REVOLVER	RIDICULOUS	RIGID
RIGOR MORTIS	RIPPED	ROBBERY	ROUTINE

S –

SABOTAGE	SCARED	SACRIFICE	SACRILEGIOUS
SAFETY	SAID	SALARY	SALUTE
SALVAGE	SANDAL	SATELLITE	SATISFACTORY
SATURDAY	SCALES	SCALLOPED	SCARCELY
SCATTER	SCENE	SCHEDULE	SCHEME
SCHIZOPHRENIA	SCIENCE	SCISSORS	SCOUT
SCRAPING	SEARCH	SECRETARY	SEDATIVE
SEDUCTION	SEGREGATE	SEIZE	SEIZURE
SEMESTER	SENSE	SENTENCE	SEPARATE
SEPARATELY	SEPARATION	SERGEANT	SETTLING
SEVERAL	SEVERED	SEWAGE	SEXUAL
SHEATH	SHERIFF	SHIMMED	SHINING
SHOWN	SHOWS	SHREWD	SHRIEK
SHRIVELED	SIEGE	SIEVE	SIGNALED
SIGNATURE	SIGNIFICANT	SILHOUETTE	SIMILAR
SIMULATE	SIMPLIFIED	SINCE	SINCERELY
SINGULAR	SIPHON	SIREN	SITTING
SKELETAL	SKETCH	SKIDDED	SLAMMED
SMELLED	SMOLDER	SMORGASBORD	SNORKEL
SOBRIETY	SOCIETY	SOLICITED	SOLICITOR
SOPHISTICATED	SOUTHERLY	SPACIOUS	SPECIALIZED
SPECIES	SPECIFIC	SPECIFY	SPECIMEN
SPEECH	SPRAIN	SQUEAL	STABILITY
STANDARD	STATEMENT	STATIONARY	STATIONERY
STATUE	STATUTORY	STEERING	STENCILED
STIFFENING	STIMULANT	STOMACH	STOPPED
STRAIGHT	STRANGULATION	STRATEGY	STRENGTH
STRICKEN	STRICTLY	STRIFE	STRIPED
STRIPPED	STRUCK	SUBDUED	SUBJECT
SUBPOENA	SUBTLE	SUCCEED	SUCCESSFUL
SUEDE	SUFFICIENT	SUFFOCATION	SUGAR

SUICIDE
SUITE
SUPERINTENDENT
SUPERIOR
SUPERSEDE
SUPERVISOR
SUPPLIES
SUPPRESS
SUPPRESSION
SUPREME
SURELY
SURFACE
SURPRISE
SURRENDER
SURREPTITIOUS
SURVEILLANCE
SUSCEPTIBLE
SUSPECT
SUSPEND
SUSPENSIONS
SUSPICION
SUSPICIOUS
SWERVE
SYMPATHY
SYMPTOM
SYNONYMOUS
SYNOPSIS

T –

TASSELED
TATTOO
TECHNICAL
TECHNIQUE
TELEGRAPH
TELEPHONE
TELEVISION
TEMPERAMENTAL
TEMPERATURE
TEMPORARY
TENANT
TENDENCY
TERMINATING
TERRITORY
TESTIMONY
TETANUS
THEATER
THEFT
THEIR
THERE
THERMOMETER
THIEVES
THOROUGH
THOUGHT
THREATEN
THRESHOLD
THROAT
THROUGH
THROWN
TISSUE
TITLE
TOBACCO
TOGETHER
TOLL
TONGUE
TONIGHT
TONSILLITIS
TOURNAMENT
TOWARD
TOWING
TRACTOR
TRAFFIC
TRAFFICKING
TRAGEDY
TRAGIC
TRAINING
TRANQUIL
TRANSACTION
TRANSFER
TRANSFERABLE
TRANSFERRED
TRANSIENT
TRANSLATION
TRANSLATOR
TRANSMIT
TRANSPORT
TRANSPOSE
TRAUMA
TREACHEROUS
TREASURER
TREASURY
TRESPASS
TRESPASSING
TRESTLE
TRIAL
TRIED
TRIES
TROLLEY
TROUBLE
TRUANCY
TRULY
TUESDAY
TUNNELED
TURQUOISE
TYPEWRITER
TYPICAL

U –

UMBRELLA
UNANIMOUS
UNCONSCIOUS
UNDERSTAND
UNDOUBTEDLY
UNIFORM
UNION
UNIQUE
UNNECESSARY
UNTIE
UNTIL
USUAL
UNUSUAL
UNUSUALLY
URGENT
URINATE
URINE
USING
USUALLY
UTENSIL
UTILITY

V –

VACANCY
VACUUM
VAGRANCY
VALIDITY
VALLEY
VALUABLE
VANDALISM
VARIETY
VEGETABLE
VEHICLE
VEIN
VELOCITY
VENGEANCE
VERBAL
VERIFIED
VERIFY
VERMIN
VERSION
VERTEBRAE
VERTICAL
VIAL
VICIOUS
VICTIM
VICTORY
VIGILANCE
VILLAGE
VIOLATION
VIOLATOR
VIOLIN
VISIBLE
VITAMIN
VIVID
VOLUME
VOLUNTARY
VOLUNTEER

W –

WAIST	WAIVE	WAREHOUSE	WARNING
WARRANT	WASTE	WATCHED	WEALTH
WEAPON	WEATHER	WEDNESDAY	WEIGHT
WEIGHTY	WEIRD	WELDER	WELFARE
WHERE	WHETHER	WHISKEY	WHOLE
WHOLLY	WHORL	WIDTH	WILLFUL
WILLFULLY	WIRY	WITNESS	WITNESSED
WITNESSES	WOMEN	WOOLEN	WOOLLY
WOUNDED	WRECK	WRESTLE	WRIST
WRIT	WRITING	WRITTEN	

X –

XRAY

Y –

YACHT	YAWN	YEAST	YEARN
YIELD	YOUNG	YOUR	YOUTHFUL

Z –

ZEALOUS	ZERO	ZIGZAG	ZINC

CHAPTER 6

ACTIVE VOICE, CHRONOLOGICAL ORDER AND WORD CHOICE

PERFORMANCE OBJECTIVES – After studying this chapter, you will be able to:

➤ Recognize and change passive voice sentence construction to active voice sentence construction.

➤ Place events in chronological order.

➤ Avoid less common words in favor of more common words.

➤ Avoid meaningless and long-winded phrases.

Grammarians say **a sentence has active voice construction when the subject of the sentence acts. A sentence has passive voice sentence construction when the subject of the sentence is acted upon.**

EXAMPLES

Active: Officer Smith found a knife. *(The subject, Officer Smith, acted.)*

Passive: A knife was found by Officer Smith. *(The subject, the knife, was acted upon)*

The most important information in a sentence should be in the beginning of that sentence for emphasis and clarity. Active voice does this. The active voice is also more concise. Look at the two examples above. Which is shorter? **Public safety reports should be written in the active voice.**

One of the worse aspects of passive voice can occur when the doer is merely left out of the sentence.

EXAMPLE

A knife was found. *(This is a proper sentence, but who does the prosecutor subpoena to testify about finding a knife?)*

PRACTICE 6.1

DIRECTIONS: Rewrite the sentences into active voice where necessary.

1. The house was burned to the ground by Gilmore.

2. Deputy Newkirk arrested Smith.

3. Paula's bicycle was stolen by Jim.

4. The suspect was taken to the county jail.

When telling any story you start at the beginning and take events in the order in which they occurred. Writing about events in the order in which they occurred is writing in chronological order. **Public safety reports should be written in chronological order.**

EXAMPLES

Bad: Smith said he discovered his television was stolen from his living room. He was only gone from his house for twenty minutes. He went to the store. He locked all his door and windows. *(Did he discover his television was stolen* **before** *he went to the store? Did he go to the store* **after** *he was gone for twenty minutes? Did he lock his doors and windows* **after** *the television was stolen?)*

Better: Smith said he locked all his doors and windows. He went to the store. He was only gone for twenty minutes. When he returned home, he discovered his television had been stolen from his living room. *(This is the natural way to tell a story.* Start at the beginning. It clears up all the questions created by the bad *example above. This is the way everyone – especially jurors – expects a story to be told.)*

PRACTICE 6.2

DIRECTIONS: Place these sentences in chronological order.

I saw a person who matched the description of the possible burglar.

I received a radio call regarding a possible burglar.

The possible burglar was described as a tall man wearing a red shirt.

I questioned the possible burglar.

We touched on the topic of word choice while discussing spelling. The easy spelling of *physical altercation* is *fight.* An even more important reason than spelling for using the more common word is that it is shorter and you will write a little less. An even more important reason than *that* for using the more common word is that it will communicate better. Many newspapers are written at about eighth grade level. Why? Because that is the reading level of most people. Even if you do have an impressive vocabulary, do you want to show it off at the expense of failing to communicate with the average juror?

Many longer, less communicative words actually have less meaning than shorter words.

EXAMPLES

The officer **contacted** the suspect. *(Did the officer telephone, personally interview or tackle the suspect? All are ways of **contacting** a person.)*

I **responded** to the accident scene. *(Did you run, drive, fly or throw up after seeing all the blood? All are responses to the scene.)*

Many other words and phrases are simply long-winded attempts to sound literary. Being literary adds nothing to your report but length.

EXAMPLES

In view of the fact that... *(Use **because**)*

At this point... *(Since reports are written in chronological order, there is no point you could be at **but** this point. Leave this phrase out entirely.)*

Some longer, less common words require you to write something you would not normally even know and raise more questions than they answer.

EXAMPLES

Bad: I **advised** the suspect of his rights. *(How do you know he was advised?* You could not have known this unless you specifically asked about it. If he spoke only Spanish he was **not** advised if you read his rights in English. Did you recite from memory or read those rights?)

Better: I **read** the suspect his rights from the departmentally issued card. (Now we know **how** he got his rights. More importantly, you can't be accused by a defense attorney of writing about something you could not possible have known.)

Bad: The witness **stated** she knew nothing about the crime. *(A statement is an intended, prepared speech. Do you know if she intended to make a statement? Was it a written or printed statement?)*

Better: The witness **said** she knew nothing about the crime. *(You know she said this.* You don't know if she intended to make a statement because that is something only she could know. We, the readers, now know how the writer got *this information. Count the number of letters in stated and said. The shorter, more common word actually tells the reader more than the longer, less common word.)*

PRACTICE 6.3

DIRECTIONS: Rewrite the sentences to make them shorter and more clear.

1. I advised subject Jones that, in reference to the aforementioned imbibing, he was no longer at liberty.

2. I stated under oath in a court of law that I had kept him under surveillance for nearly a fortnight.

3. I observed the fiery exchange of words between the adult male protagonists.

4. I detected the odor of smoldering *Cannabis sativa L.* and noted on my chronometer the hour as two o'clock in the afternoon.

CHAPTER 7

PARAGRAPHING, JARGON AND SLANG, FACTS/INFERENCES/OPINIONS

PERFORMANCE OBJECTIVES – After studying this chapter, you will be able to:

➤ Correctly divide public safety reports into paragraphs.

➤ Identify and correct usage of jargon and slang except when directly quoted

➤ Differentiate between facts, inferences and opinions and know which to use.

The idea of paragraphing is to put related sentences together and start new paragraphs when you start a new series of related sentences. In public safety report writing this means you will have separate paragraphs for: (1) how you got involved, (2) your observations and/or actions, (3) the victim's statement (if any), (4) the suspect's statement (if any) and (5) each witness' statement.

Within any one of the five separate categories of paragraphs above, indent at the beginning of a new topic to start a new paragraph if a paragraph gets too long. *Between* the five categories of paragraphs above, skip a space to let the reader know there has been a major shift in your telling of the story.

EXAMPLE

In response to a radio call I drove to the scene and met the victim there. (This first paragraph always tells why and how you became involved.) Smith, the victim, essentially said he locked all his doors and windows. He went to the store. He was only gone for twenty minutes. When he returned home, he discovered his television had been stolen from his living room. *(The victim's statement and **only** the victim's statement is in this paragraph. The victim's statement is in **chronological order as it occurred to the victim**. Because it started with "Smith said..." the reader will automatically assume everything here was said by Smith. There is no need to repeatedly write "Smith said..." It is also unnecessary to write "I asked..." and "He said..." over and over. Generally, no one cares what you asked.)*

I saw pry marks on the back door by the latch and wood chips on the floor below the pry marks. *(Your observations and/or actions belong in a separate paragraph. The order of the **paragraphs** is dictated by the order of events as they occurred to you, the writer.)*

Jones, the neighbor immediately to the south of Smith, said essentially that she saw Smith leave his house. About five minutes later she saw a small white pickup truck parked in front of Smith's house. *(The witness' statement and **only the** witness' statement belongs in this separate paragraph if there is a known witness.)*

(In the above example it is assumed there is a separate place on a public safety report form to enter more complete identifying information on the location, item(s) stolen, victim, witness, etc.)

The order of the paragraphs is dictated by the chronology of the events. In the above example the writer got a radio call, met the victim, got the victim's story, saw the pry marks and got the witness' story *in that order*. If the events had occurred in a different order, the paragraphs would have had to be written in a different order to remain chronological. **Within each paragraph the events are also in chronological order.**

The victim may have started telling you his story by saying, "Someone broke into my house and stole my television." That was not the first part of his story, but he considered it the most important part, so he told you that first. It will be your job to put events into chronological order for the victim. It will make far better sense to your superiors, prosecuting attorneys and jury if you do.

If you started each person's statement with *"(Name) **essentially** said...,"* no one could accuse you of misrepresenting the other person's statement. There was no need to write down *everything* you were told. If someone told you he needed to use the restroom, you weren't not going to write that down. What you **did** need to record was the essence of what a person told you.

Every profession has its own terminology. This terminology is completely understandable only to those in that profession. This is jargon. **Public safety jargon is unacceptable in public safety reports** unless it is part of an exact and necessary quote (see earlier section on quotation marks).

Jargon is unacceptable because public safety reports are not read only by people in public safety work. Abbreviations which could only be easily deciphered by someone in public safety work would qualify as jargon, as would all radio codes and numbers of criminal code statutes. Write your reports to the readers who are least sophisticated about the criminal justice, public safety and the court system. Write your reports so *jurors* can understand them. All others will be able to understand them as well.

EXAMPLES

Bad: I arrested him for **459.** (**459** is the California Penal Code section number for burglary.)

Better: I arrested him for burglary. (Though this is longer it will be understood by everybody, not just California cops)

Bad: I was **10-4** on that. (**10-4** is almost universal among two-way radio users as an acknowledgement indicating that the previous radio message was understood. Not everybody uses two-way radios, however.)

Better: I understood that.

Slang, like jargon, is understood by only certain people. Slang is spoken among all those in a sub-culture, not a profession. Like jargon, slang is unacceptable in public safety reports with one exception. **Use slang in public safety reports only when giving an exact and necessary quote**. (This was previously discussed when quotation mark rules and examples were given. Review those.)

PRACTICE 7.1

DIRECTIONS: Eliminate jargon and slang as needed in the following sentences.

1. It looked like neither of the victims needed to be sewed up.

2. His record showed a previous arrest as a flasher.

3. He said he was wasted.

4. It was a quarter-sized package of cocaine.

Facts are statements upon which virtually everyone can agree. Inferences are facts derived from other facts. Opinions are statements based upon no facts. Opinions are conclusionary and may raise that objection from the defense attorney when you are testifying if you try to use them.

EXAMPLES

Opinion: His actions were suspicious. *(No facts are presented. Conclusionary.)*

Fact: He stood in front of a jewelry store. He wore an overcoat despite the ninety degree weather. When another person approached the store he walked away and then returned. *(Any two people watching this person would be able to agree on these statements.)*

Inference: He stood in front of a jewelry store. He wore an overcoat despite the ninety degree weather. When another person approached the store he walked away and then returned. **His actions were suspicious**. *(The final statement, by itself, is nothing more than an opinion. But, when several facts precede the final statement, it becomes an inference, a fact derived from other facts.)* **Inferences are acceptable and sometimes absolutely necessary in public safety reports. Public safety reports should consist of facts and inferences. Opinions should not be in public safety reports.**

PRACTICE 7.2

DIRECTIONS: Label each of the following sentences an opinion, a fact or an **inference.**

1. Most crimes involve illegal narcotics.

2. Smith said essentially that he was hit in the head by a thrown rock.

3. The suspect made a furtive movement.

4. Because the suspect drove poorly, displayed poor balance and coordination, had slurred speech and the odor of an alcoholic beverage on his breath, I concluded he was driving under the influence of alcohol.

CHAPTER 8

THE PROCESS OF PUBLIC SAFETY REPORT WRITING

PERFORMANCE OBJECTIVES – After studying this chapter, you will be able to:

➤ Take field notes.

➤ Describe the uses of field notes.

➤ Tell which types of information are appropriate in field notes.

➤ Conduct field interviews.

➤ Describe which types of information are appropriate in crime scene notes.

➤ Explain how public safety reports are used and who the users are.

➤ Give the characteristics of good public safety reports.

➤ Tell what questions are answered by complete public safety reports.

Human memory is not perfect. It is usually necessary to take notes of events we wish to later recall exactly. These notes are often referred to as field notes because they are made "in the field." **Field notes are mere abbreviations of what was actually said, seen or done** because few of us can write all things down as quickly as we hear, see or do them.

Field notes are primarily for the use of the reporting officer, not the prosecuting attorney, judge or jury. Field notes are, therefore, the exception to the rule concerning writing public safety reports in complete sentences with standard abbreviations. Just as you take lecture notes that are not complete sentences in class to later refresh your memory before a test, you **take field notes to later refresh your memory when writing reports.**

Ever try to use someone else's class notes? Weren't you frustrated if you couldn't understand them or thankful if you could? Though non-standard abbreviations and non-sentences may be used in field notes, make sure at least some other officer can understand them in case something happens to you.

Good field notes help eliminate the need to re-contact the parties involved just as good class notes help eliminate the need to later ask your instructors about earlier lectures.

Because of the imperfection of human memory, **good field notes** (or good class notes) **will provide better recollection than mere memory alone.**

What types of information should be included in field notes? What types of things will you later need for writing your report? **Minimally, your field notes will need to include information about:**

> **Suspects** *(What are their names? addresses? descriptions?)*
>
> **Victims** *(You need work **and** home information for detectives and subpoenas.)*
>
> **Witnesses** *(Virtually the same information needed for victims is needed witnesses.)*
>
> **Date(s) and time(s) of occurrence** *(It happened between when and when?)*
>
> **Exact location of occurrence** *(Necessary to establish jurisdiction and possible later crime scene or accident reconstruction.)*
>
> **Any other important information** *(You can't include **everything** but you'll never have a better chance to get all important information than that first time at the scene. When in doubt, make an error of too much information instead of too little.)*

When interviewing people in the field, put them at ease. Establish rapport if time allows by showing some personal interest in them. Try to become a person to them, not just an officer.

EXAMPLES

> **Ask:** Would you be more comfortable sitting down? *(This **asking**, as opposed to **ordering**, helps eliminate the intimidating effect of the badge and uniform.)*
>
> **Explain:** I know you're a bit shaken by this but the information I need from you might help us recover your property and catch the thief. *(Explaining your purpose and showing concern for a victim's feelings will net you more information than a bullying and unconcerned approach. That's even true when talking to suspects.)*

Ask questions which do not imply answers and which require more than yes or no answers.

EXAMPLES

> **Bad:** Was he tall? *(Needs only a yes or no and neither tells you much)*
> **Better:** What was his height?
>
> **Bad:** What kind of weapon did he have? *(Implies that there was a weapon)*
> **Better:** Was there anything in his hands?

Allow people to tell their complete stories once without taking notes. Some people get nervous about you "putting it down in black and white" and might prefer that their statements be "off the record." You also don't want to frustrate them by slowing them down. You can't write as quickly as they speak. After they've blurted out their emotional (rather than factual) and rambling (rather than chronologically ordered) story once, get out your notebook and get the facts you need in the order in which they actually occurred.

Tell them you can't possibly remember all that they said and start writing down (in note style) the important information for your later report. This time go at your pace. Now you'll have the advantage of hearing their story twice. If there are contradictions, note them and ask about them. They may just be emotionally distraught or they may be lying. Either condition tells prosecuting attorneys something about what kind of witnesses they'll be.

Let them do most of the talking. You can't learn much if you are talking all the time. Nothing encourages others to talk more than giving them opportunities to talk.

If your note taking is done at the crime scene itself, you will need to record **in addition to the above field notes:**

1. **Significant conditions present at the time of your arrival**. *(What did you see, smell and hear when you got there?)*

2. **A chronological account of your actions until you were relieved.** *(What did you do first? second? third?)*

3. **Any identification or handling of evidence**. *(Necessary for the "chain of custody" of evidence)*

Public safety reports are used to:

Record facts into a permanent record. *(Your report will stay on file forever.)*

Provide coordination of follow-up activities and investigative leads. *(Any report of a crime not immediately solved will be forwarded to detectives who will rely on your report to tell them what happened.)*

Provide the basis for prosecution (and sometimes the defense as well). *(The prosecuting attorney will decide whether or not to issue a complaint based on what you wrote, not on what you **know** about the case. In most jurisdictions the defense attorney is entitled to a complete copy of your report. A poor report may actually provide the basis of the suspect's defense.)*

Provide a source for officer evaluation. *(Supervisors will not always be at your incident scenes. They will know the quality of your work **primarily** by what you write.)*

Provide statistical data. *(Need more officers? That need must be established statistically before you will get any new help doing your job. Those statistics come from your reports.)*

Provide reference material. *(You will refresh your memory from your report before testifying. Others may even use your report as the basis for lawsuits against others or **you.**)*

The characteristics of good public safety reports are:

Accuracy *(Accomplished through noun specificity, past tense, proper punctuation, use of first person, proper use of modifiers.)*

Conciseness *(Accomplished through the use of active voice, good word choices.)*

Clarity *(Accomplished through the proper use of comparative modifies, subject-verb agreement, pronoun-antecedent agreement, chronological order, proper paragraphing, elimination of jargon/slang except as necessary.)*

Legibility *(Accomplished by using only capital letters.)*

Objectivity *(Accomplished through the use of facts and inferences, not opinions.)*

Correct grammar *(Accomplished through the use of complete and proper sentences.)*

Correct spelling *(Accomplished through a lot of memorizing and/or the constant use of a dictionary.)*

Completeness *(Accomplished by making sure your report answers these questions: Who? What? Where? When? Why? How?)*

ANSWERS TO PRACTICES

Chapter 1

NOUNS AND PRONOUNS

PRACTICE 1.1

1. <u>Sam</u> gave the <u>evidence</u> to <u>Frank</u>.

2. <u>George</u> got the <u>knife</u> from <u>Larry</u>.

3. <u>Bob</u> is a good <u>officer</u>.

4. The <u>burglar</u> was <u>mad</u> but decided to tell the <u>truth</u> anyway.

PRACTICE 1.2

1. The <u>truck</u> was blue. (***Vehicle*** *includes virtually everything with wheels.* ***Motor vehicle*** *is slightly more specific but still includes everything from motor scooters to tractors.*)

2. The <u>shooting</u> took place on Main Street. (***Assault*** *includes everything from a swung fist to most types of violent murders.*)

3. The <u>man</u> wore a blue shirt. (***Male*** *includes baby boys, old men and all males in between.*)

4. His <u>breath</u> smelled like an alcoholic beverage. (***Person*** *includes one's clothing. You probably want to prove there is an alcoholic beverage* ***in*** *him, not* ***on*** *him.*)

PRACTICE 1.3

1. Members of the teenage <u>gang</u> interrupted the party.

2. He shot into the <u>crowd</u> of shoppers.

3. The motorcycle <u>club</u> included several ex-felons.

4. The traffic <u>jam</u> caused numerous accidents.

PRACTICE 1.4

1. <u>He</u> asked <u>his</u> younger sister to watch <u>them</u> for <u>him</u>.

2. <u>They</u> said <u>those</u> were the suspect's pants.

3. <u>You</u> are the first to use <u>it</u>.

4. <u>He</u> said <u>he</u> had seized <u>them</u> as evidence.

PRACTICE 1.5

1. <u>Ours</u> is better than <u>yours</u>.

2. The knife used in the murder was <u>hers</u>.

PRACTICE 1.6

1. Tom and <u>she</u> saw the marijuana plants. *(**She** saw, not **her** saw.)*

2. My partner and <u>I</u> made three arrests last week. *(**I** made three arrests last week, not **me** made three arrests last week.)*

3. The two suspects, Smith and <u>she</u>, were at the same house. *(**She** was at the house, not **her** was at the house.)*

4. <u>He</u> and I will take that call right away. *(**He** will take that call, not **him** will take that call.)*

PRACTICE 1.7

1. Tom and <u>I</u> went to the suspect's house together. *(You'd never say **myself** went to, would you?)*

2. The accident was seen by Parker and <u>me</u>.

PRACTICE 1.8

1. He knows <u>something</u>.

2. <u>Everyone</u> was in complete agreement.

3. He was willing to sell to <u>anyone</u> who asked.

4. <u>Anybody</u> could have seen it.

PRACTICE 1.9

1. There was a brown dog in the car on the seat.

   OR

   The car had a brown dog on the seat.

2. Officer Black went into his house with Officer White.

   OR

   Officer Black went into his house. Officer White went with him.

3. "You no longer have a job," the mayor said to the chief.

   OR

   The chief no longer had a job. He was told so by the mayor.

4. The two witnesses saw the robbers leave the building and get into their car.

   OR

   The robbers left the building and got into their car according to the two witnesses.

   These are just some of several different ways to rewrite the sentences and make the pronoun references clear.

Chapter 2
VERBS AND AGREEMENT

PRACTICE 2.1

1. He <u>is</u> a famous jewel thief.

2. Jimmy <u>should have been prepared</u>.

3. Dave <u>pursued</u> the getaway car.

4. I <u>ran</u> to the hurt victim.

PRACTICE 2.2

1. He <u>started</u> the car.

2. I <u>investigated</u> the accident.

3. They <u>ran</u> away.

4. We <u>went</u> to lunch.

PRACTICE 2.3

1. She <u>drove</u> the car.

2. I <u>brought</u> the coffee you asked for.

3. He <u>broke</u> the window.

4. The officer <u>found</u> the knife.

PRACTICE 2.4

1. **I** arrested Harrington.

2. **I** pursued the red Honda.

3. **I** saw the crime occur.

4. **I** wrote the report.

PRACTICE 2.5

1. <u>Their uniforms</u> are blue.

2. <u>Detectives</u> are usually experienced patrol officers. (***Officers*** *is also a noun but not all nouns or pronouns are the subjects of sentences.*)

3. <u>The burglars</u> specialized in doctors' offices.

4. <u>My arm</u> is still sore.

PRACTICE 2.6

1. Are there <u>two motorcycle</u> officers working today?

2. Into the room burst <u>the suspect</u>.

3. Where are <u>officers Smith and Jones</u>?

4. From out of the clouds came <u>the helicopter</u>.

PRACTICE 2.7

1. He <u>was</u> in charge.

2. I <u>was</u> frightened.

3. We <u>were</u> late.

4. They <u>were</u> in trouble.

PRACTICE 2.8

1. The lieutenant, followed by his sergeants, <u>was</u> in the parade. *(**The lieutenant** is the subject of the sentence and it is singular.)*

2. Everybody <u>was</u> working hard. *(**Everybody** is an indefinite pronoun.)*

3. The mob of looters <u>was</u> setting stores on fire. *(**Mob** is a collective noun.)*

4. The parked cars and the motorcycle <u>were</u> involved in the accident. *(This would have been a plural subject even without **and** because **cars** is plural.)*

PRACTICE 2.9

1. Officers must remember to turn off <u>their</u> radios before entering the building.

2. An officer never forgets <u>his</u> (or <u>her</u>) first arrest.

Chapter 3
MODIFIERS AND SENTENCE STRUCTURE

PRACTICE 3.1

1. <u>The</u> victim was <u>pretty</u>.

2. <u>The two</u> burglars were young. *(In this case, **young** is a noun. In the phrase **young boys**, **young** would be an adjective. Remember, some words can be different parts of speech depending on their usage.)*

3. The youngest suspect wore purple shoes.

4. The best shooter in the group was the lieutenant.

PRACTICE 3.2

1. He did his work efficiently. *(**Efficiently** modifies **did**, a verb.)*

2. She was arrested twice for drunk driving. *(**Twice** modifies **arrested**, a verb. **Words giving number are not always adverbs.** In **she has two arrests**, the word **two** is an **adjective** modifying **arrests**, a noun. Words giving numbers are adverbs when they tell **how often.**)*

3. The very young suspect wore brightly colored shoes. *(**Very** modifies **young**, an adjective, and **brightly** modifies **colored**, an adjective.)*

4. I will gladly never do it again.

PRACTICE 3.3

1. He ate quickly. *(**Ate** is the word being modified. **Ate** is a verb. An adjective cannot modify a verb but an adverb can. **Quickly** is an adverb. **Fast** and **quick** are adjectives.)*

2. The chemicals smelled awfully. *(**Smelled**, a verb, is properly modified by **awfully**, an adverb, not **awful**, an adjective.)*

3. The heavily armed suspects resisted arrest.

4. His mood changed suddenly.

PRACTICE 3.4

1. She is the most intelligent person on the police department. *(Comparison of three or more. There is no such word as **intelligentest.**)*

2. Of the two of them, I think Joe is taller. *(Comparison of two. **Tallest** would only be used if three or more were compared.)*

3. Officer Kearns does his work more efficiently than Officer Herbert. *(The answer is not **more efficient** because **efficient** is an adjective. What we need here is a modifier telling **how**, an adverb. **Efficiently** ends in–ly. Therefore, it is an adverb. The word **more** is needed to show the comparison because there is no such word as **efficienter**.)*

4. Compared to Pat and Dave, he reloads his pistol most quickly. *(This is a comparison of three or more so you can eliminate **more quickly** which compares*

*only two qualities. That leaves **quickest** and **most quickly.** We are looking for a word to modify **reloads,** a verb. Do adjectives modify verbs? No. **Quickly** is an adverb. Adverbs modify verbs. **Most** is needed to show the comparison of three or more qualities.)*

PRACTICE 3.5

1. He saw the bank as he rounded the corner.

2. The knife seemed small when it was looked at a second time.

3. The marijuana found outside the car was wrapped in paper.

4. Last night he said he would paint the house.

    These are only examples of several different ways to eliminate confusion in each of the above sentences.

PRACTICE 3.6

1. The burglar broke the window and entered the house. *(**The burglar broke the window** could be a sentence by itself but **and entered the house** could not be a sentence because it has no subject.)*

2. She noticed the blue car weaving down the road.

3. OK as is – two complete sentences.

4. The victim was afraid to testify after she was threatened.

    OR

    After she was threatened, the victim was afraid to testify.

PRACTICE 3.7

1. OK as is. (It is not a run-on because **became suspicious and phoned the police** is not a sentence. A run-on sentence contains two separate sentences which are incorrectly made into one. It would be better, however, to break this into two or three sentences for report writing purposes. Example: The pawn broker saw the suspects. He became suspicious and called the police.)

2. Dave shot his pistol and then cleaned it. *(This is **not** a run-on sentence. A run-on sentence must contain more than one sentence. **Then cleaned it** is not a sentence.)*

3. The burglar was finally booked. I went home to bed.

4. The suspect appeared in court. He acted nervously.

PRACTICE 3.8

1. He left his fingerprints at the scene. I found several of them.

2. OK as is – **not** a comma splice. *(Comma splices involve two or more complete sentences. **Having much work to do** is not a sentence.)*

3. The burglars entered the building. They opened every office door.

    OR

    The burglars entered the building and opened every office door. *(This sentence is not a run-on because **and opened every office door** is not a sentence.)*

4. OK as is.

Chapter 4
PUNCTUATION

PRACTICE 4.1

1. Did you last arrest Smith in March? Was it during April? *(Placing a comma after **March** in the original sentence is technically correct for writing **prose**. For report writing purposes however, the comma and **or** produce a run-on sentence because you can –and therefore should – make two complete sentences from it.)*

2. Kathy, a five-year veteran, was awarded a lifesaving medal.

3. Patrick, you have done a fine job.

4. After the shooting, all the people were interviewed.

PRACTICE 4.2

1. He lived at 1234 D E. Fourth, Boulevard, California. *(There really **is** such a place as Boulevard, California. Without knowing this, and without commas, deciphering this sentence would be difficult. Even if you **did** know there was a Boulevard, California, deciphering an address of someone from Japan or Ethiopia without commas is nearly impossible.)*

2. The date was January 18, 1949. *(You cannot rely on spacing in handwritten documents to convey true meanings. Merely leaving a space between numbers leaves too much to chance. Commas clear up any possible misunderstandings.)*

3. The stolen sweater is blue, red, yellow, and green. *(The comma after yellow is optional. The reader has already slowed in reading this series of things because of the word **and** before the last item in the series.)*

4. OK as is.

PRACTICE 4.3

1. He was a fine officer.

2. She worked and worked on that case. *(A comma is only needed in a series of three or more things **not** separated by the word **and.**)*

3. Detective Hoffman got angry and broke his pencil.

4. OK as is.

PRACTICE 4.4

1. They're having fun in their boat over there.

2. He went to the Sea 'n' Sea Sport Shop. *(**A** and **d** are both missing from the word **and.**)*

3. We're going to Rick's house for the Class of '82 reunion.

4. Haven't you got anything better to do at ten o'clock? *(**O'clock** is a shortened version of **the clock.**)*

PRACTICE 4.5

1. It's hot here and I miss San Diego's cool ocean breezes. *(It's stands for it is. There is a letter missing so an apostrophe is required. The apostrophe in San Diego's shows possession. Incidentally, this is a run-on sentence.)*

2. OK as is.

3. OK as is.

4. Its coat is shaggy and it's ugly. (**Its** is a possessive pronoun, no apostrophe required. **It's** stands for **it is**. The apostrophe is needed to *show there is a letter missing. This is also a run-on sentence.)*

PRACTICE 4.6

1. It was Willis' car.

2. The two repossessors' papers were in order.

3. The three officers' pistols were inspected.

4. The duchess' limousine was black.

PRACTICE 4.7

1. The hay bales were not theirs. *(Plurals are formed with apostrophes only if they are plurals of letters, numbers and figures. **Bales** needs no apostrophe where it is merely a plural. **Theirs** is a possessive pronoun.)*

2. There's no difference between Shelly's and Ann's pistols. *(**There's** stands for **there is**. The apostrophe is needed. The apostrophes in **Shelly's** and **Ann's** show possession. **Pistols** is merely a plural of something other than a letter, number or figure. No apostrophe is needed.)*

3. The criminals' faces were not visible to the witnesses.

4. Your brother's sister had several ?'s on her test paper. *(**Brother's** shows possession and **?'s** is the plural of the figure?)*

PRACTICE 4.8

1. The suspect said his <u>Miranda</u> rights were violated.

2. The victim was found in a ditch.

> OR *(if it is important to the case)*

The victim, a prostitute, was found in a ditch.

3. I found twelve balloons of heroin in the suspect's pockets.

4. Officer Jones read Brown his rights. ***(Brown was read his rights by Officer Jones before he was questioned*** *is passive voice.)*

PRACTICE 4.9

1. The suspect, after seeing the evidence, confessed.

   > OR

   After seeing the evidence, the suspect confessed.

   > OR *(if seeing the evidence first was not important)*

   The suspect confessed.

2. There were twenty-one ounce vials.

   > OR

   There were twenty one-ounce vials. *(In the first sentence, there were 21 vials of an ounce each. In the second sentence, there were only 20 vials of one ounce each. The correct answer depends on how you first read the practice sentence.)*

3. My sergeant headed up the investigative team. *(Simply leave out unimportant information.)*

4. OK as is, assuming you didn't mean **through** August 22. *(The hyphen substitutes for the word **to** not **through**.)*

PRACTICE 4.10

1. Dorie said, "I'm not talking without my lawyer."

2. The victim saw the suspect entering a window. He yelled at him. *(Should be two sentences. Is **him** a confusing pronoun?)*

3. OK as is.

4. The traffic officer looked at the accident scene. He saw a skid mark he had not seen before.

PRACTICE 4.11

1. Leave this quote out of the report entirely. It is almost certainly not essential to any case.

2. I searched the car within the guidelines of U.S. v. Ross.

    OR

    I searched the car within the guidelines of *U.S.* v. *Ross*.

3. Rick said, "I only roughed her up."

    OR

    Rick said he only "roughed her up." *(The first is better because it is an admission which should be entirely quoted. The second is acceptable where the exact quote is not available but where Rick definitely used the phrase **roughed her up** which is slang.)*

4. OK as is. *(It helps prove the suspect is guilty by showing his knowledge that what you found was, in fact, marijuana.)*

Chapter 5

CAPITALIZATION, ABBREVIATION AND SPELLING

PRACTICE 5.1

1. THE SUSPECT WAS GONE WHEN I ARRIVED. *(Some agencies use GOA for "gone on arrival." If you had no idea what GOA stood for, don't feel bad. Most jurors wouldn't know either. That's one of the points of this practice.)*

2. I GAVE THE EVIDENCE TO LT. JOHNSON OF THE B_____ P_____ D_____ . *(See how capitalizing everything kept you from having to decide whether or not to capitalize Johnson's title? How many police departments can you think of which could be called BPD? Is it possible it doesn't stand for any police department? That's the point. There are far too many possibilities. Only one such possibility in your area, you say?*

    *What will happen if your report goes with the appeal of this case to U.S. Supreme Court? Do you want those justices to **guess** what BPD stands for?)*

3. HENRY ST. INTERSECTS BOWLING DR. *(No problem with abbreviations here and capitalizing everything takes care of the question of whether or not to capitalize street names.)*

4. HE WAS ASSIGNED TO THE CRIME SUPPRESSION UNIT? THE CALI-
FORNIA STATE UNIVERSITY? *(Who knows what CSU stands for?* **Spell it
out instead of abbreviating if there is any doubt that any juror will misun-
derstand the abbreviation.)**

Chapter 6

ACTIVE AND PASSIVE VOICE, CHRONOLOGICAL ORDER AND WORD CHOICE

PRACTICE 6.1

1. Gilmore burned the house to the ground.

2. OK as is.

3. Jim stole Paula's bicycle.

4. This is the worst kind of passive voice. Though the sentence is grammatically
correct, the reader has no way of knowing who took the suspect to the county
jail.

PRACTICE 6.2

I received a radio call regarding a possible burglar. He was described as a
tall man wearing a red shirt. I saw a person matching his description. I
questioned him. *(Notice that the use of correct chronological order
allowed us to use pronouns instead of "the possible burglar" without
confusion. This made the correct version significantly shorter than the
original.)*

PRACTICE 6.3

1. I told Jones he was under arrest for drunk driving (or driving under the influence
of alcohol.)

2. I testified that I watched him for almost two weeks.

3. I saw the two men argue.

4. I smelled burning marijuana at 1400 hours.

*(If some of these were difficult for you, good. Now you know how
others feel when you don't write simply.)*

Chapter 7

PARAGRAPHING, JARGON AND SLANG, FACTS/INFERENCES/OPINIONS

PRACTICE 7.1

1. Neither victim appeared to need stitches for their wounds. *(Don't use **sutures**. That's medical jargon.)*

2. His record showed a previous arrest for indecent exposure *(Or some other term for **flasher** understood by all.)*

3. He said he was "wasted." *(It's assumed here the suspect is being exactly quoted.)*

4. It was a package of cocaine of a size normally purchased for $25. *(This is still an awkward sentence for a police report because it will require a lot of expertise on your part before most courts will let you say this from the witness stand. At least it's better than **quarter-sized** which most jurors will think is something the size of a 25 cent coin. Quarter, meaning $25, is (or was) southern California drug slang. It may not apply to other regions.)*

   *   These are only some of the ways to eliminate jargon and slang. Your answers may be correct without being exactly like these.

PRACTICE 7.2

1. Because it is written without supporting facts, this is an opinion. It does not belong in a police report.

2. It may be used in a police report. Wouldn't any two people hearing Smith agree he said this? It is a fact.

3. This is an opinion. It does not belong in a police report. A description of the actual movement would be factual. **He made a quick movement with his right hand toward his waistband** would be a fact. Any two people seeing this movement would agree he did this.

4. Though this is a run-on sentence, it is an inference. Its several-sentence equivalent would be appropriate in a police report.

SAMPLE REPORTS

SAMPLE BAD REPORT*

[The standard heading of the actual report showed it was for an arrest of two men for being drunk in public. They were fully identified. A juvenile was detained. It occurred on 2-16-99, at 12:35 am at 400 S. Cherokee.]

FURTHER DETAILS:

On 2-16-99, at 12:35 AM, this officer, while in the parking lot of Tic Toc Market at First and Cherokee, was contacted by an unknown named subject who advised this officer that in the alleyway at 400 South Cherokee two subjects were engaged in a fist fight.

This officer responded to that location and upon arrival observed two subjects to be facing each other as if they were going to begin to fight. This officer exited the police vehicle and upon doing so subject YOUNG turned and ran eastbound through the alley. At this time this officer responded to subject WELLS who was standing at the location and this officer yelled at subject YOUNG to freeze and to return to this officer. YOUNG appeared to be extremely intoxicated and turned around and ran back towards this officer.

At this point this officer asked subject WELLS what transpired and subject WELLS simply did not answer this officer. It should be noted that at this time, Officer Brown has arrived at the scene and both subjects YOUNG and WELLS were once again facing each other. This officer heard the subject WELLS state to YOUNG, "Okay, if you want to fight, let's go!" at which time subject WELLS took a karate type stance, as if he was preparing for a fight. At this time this officer stepped between both subjects drawing the baton from the baton ring and ordering subject YOUNG to the rear of a vehicle which was parked in the alley approximately five feet away. Due to the fact that subject YOUNG was extremely intoxicated this officer placed subject YOUNG under arrest for being drunk in public. The subject was handcuffed and placed in the rear of this officer's vehicle. It should also be noted that subject WELLS was also extremely intoxicated and was in fact taken into custody by Officer Brown upon request of this officer. Subject WELLS at this time was placed in the rear of Officer Black's vehicle and then replaced into Officer Green's vehicle.

It should be noted that while both subjects were facing each other this officer got a chance to look at subject WELLS' face and also subject YOUNG's face. It should be noted that on WELLS' face there was a small cut below the right eye which appeared as if subject WELLS had been struck by the subject YOUNG. This officer had information from the subject, who informed this officer of the fight, that both subjects had already in fact been fighting.

It should be noted that subject YOUNG had a reddening mark under one of his eyes which appeared that subject YOUNG had been struck by the subject WELLS. While this officer was attempting to conduct an investigation by contacting witnesses, contact was made with suspect LIBBY PINK.

This officer asked LIBBY PINK if she had seen any actions that had taken place at that location at which time she stated no she did not and that she wasn't going to say anything. At this time this officer asked for identification from the subject LIBBY PINK, at which time she stated that she did not have any and that she would not answer any questions asked by this officer. It should be noted that subject LIBBY PINK appeared to be very young and attempts were made to obtain identification and also her age. The subject, LIBBY PINK stated to this officer that she had driven to the location in a vehicle and would supply this officer with no further information other than her home phone number. This officer contacted witness AL PINK, who advised this officer that the suspect in question was in fact only 16 years old and he had thought that she was at a movie. Due to this fact the subject was taken into custody by this officer for violation of curfew.

The suspect was transported to the city police department where she was placed in a juvenile detention room. The suspect's father was then contacted by this officer and advised of the circumstances and suspect LIBBY PINK was released to the custody of AL PINK. It should be noted that a juvenile contact report was completed on this subject by the undersigned.

It should be noted that both suspects involved in the fight were transported to the city police department where they were released to the custody of the jailer. No further action was taken by this officer.

It should by noted that at no time during the confrontation in the alley did this officer or any other officers become involved in any type of altercation with either suspects WELLS or YOUNG.

*Source for the SAMPLE BAD REPORT and SAMPLE GOOD RE-PORT: *It's Easy to Write Better Police Reports* by Devallis Rutledge. Printed by the California Commission on Peace Officer Standards and Training as part of their Exemplary Training Program. Not copyrighted.

SAMPLE GOOD REPORT

In the parking lot of Tic Toc Market at First and Cherokee a man told me that in the alley at 400 S. Cherokee two men were fighting.

I went there and saw two men facing each other as if they were going to fight. As I left my police car, YOUNG turned and ran east through the alley. I walked to WELLS and I yelled at YOUNG to stop and return. YOUNG appeared to be extremely intoxicated; he turned around and ran back toward me.

I asked WELLS what happened. He did not answer. Officer Brown had arrived at the scene and YOUNG and WELLS were facing each other again. I heard WELLS say to YOUNG: "Okay, if you want to fight, let's go!" Then WELLS took a karate-type stance, as if he were preparing for a fight. I stepped in between both men, drew my baton, and ordered YOUNG to the rear of a parked vehicle about five feet away. Because YOUNG was extremely intoxicated, I arrested him for being drunk in public. I handcuffed him and put him in the back seat of my police car. WELLS was also extremely intoxicated. At my request, Officer Brown arrested him and put him in Officer Black's police car and then into Officer Green's.

While YOUNG and WELLS were facing each other, I had seen their faces. I saw a small cut below WELLS' right eye. It appeared that YOUNG might have struck him. I had information from the man who told me of the fight that both men had been fighting.

YOUNG had a reddening mark under one of his eyes; apparently WELLS had struck him. While I was talking to witnesses, I spoke to LIBBY PINK.

I asked LIBBY PINK if she had seen what had happened. She said, "No," and that she wasn't going to say anything. I asked her for identification. She said she had none and would not answer any questions. She appeared to be young, so I asked her for identification and asked her age. She said she had driven there and would give no further information, other than her home phone number. I called AL PINK, who said that LIBBY was 16 years old, and that he thought she was at a movie. I detained LIBBY PINK for curfew violation.

I drove LIBBY PINK to the police department and put her in a juvenile detention room. I then phoned her father and told him what had happened. I released LIBBY to him, and completed a juvenile contact report.

Both suspects involved in the fight were taken to the city police department where they were released to the custody of the jailer. I took no further action.

Neither I nor any other officer was involved in any kind of altercation with WELLS or YOUNG in the alley.

The best way to compare the two samples above is to look at each sentence of the original report, then look at that same sentence in the SAMPLE GOOD REPORT. To make this comparison easier, Rutledge used the same paragraph divisions.

SAMPLE BETTER REPORT

In the parking lot of Tic Toc Market at First and Cherokee a man told me that two men were fighting in the alley at 400 S. Cherokee.

I drove there and saw two men facing each other as if they were going to fight or continue fighting. Under the right eye of one man (later identified as WELLS) was a small cut. Under one of the eyes *[which one?]* of the other man (later identified as YOUNG) was a reddening mark. As I left my police car YOUNG turned and ran east through the alley. I walked to WELLS and I yelled at YOUNG to stop and return. *[Here should be some recording of objective symptoms of intoxication for each of them.]* YOUNG turned and ran back towards me.

I asked WELLS what had happened. He did not answer.

Officers Brown arrived. YOUNG and WELLS faced each other again.

WELLS said, "Okay, if you want to fight, let's go."

WELLS took a karate-type stance as if preparing to fight. I stepped between both men, drew my baton and ordered YOUNG to the rear of a parked vehicle about five feet away. I arrested YOUNG for being drunk in public. I handcuffed him and put him in the back seat of my police car. At my request, Officer Brown arrested WELLS for being drunk in public and put him in Officer Black's police car and then into Officer Green's. *[When did they get here?]*

Neither I nor any other officer was involved in any use of force with WELLS or YOUNG in the alley.

Both suspects involved in the fight were taken to the city jail *[by whom?]* and were released to the city jailer.

[Since LIBBY PINK contributed nothing to the arrest of the two men, it would have been best to handle her curfew violation as a totally separate report.]

LIBBY PINK said she had not seen anything and was not going to say anything further. She claimed to have no identification. She would give no information other than her phone number.

Because LIBBY PINK appeared to be under 18 and it was past curfew, I phoned the number she gave and spoke to AL PINK, her father.

AL PINK said LIBBY was 16 years old and he thought she was at a movie.

I detained LIBBY PINK for curfew violation and drove her to the police department. I put her in a juvenile detention room. I phoned her father and told him what happened. When he arrived at the police department I released LIBBY to him and completed a juvenile contact report.

> **Author's Note**: This is still not a great report. The bracketed notes in italics within this last report point out problems which cannot be resolved with the information supplied. Nevertheless, by separating LIBBY PINK from the drunk arrests and placing items into chronologically ordered and related paragraphs it is hoped that better sense was made here of what we were given.

GLOSSARY

ABBREVIATION – A shortened word ending with a period. Example: *St.* is an abbreviation for *street*.

ABSTRACT NOUN – A word for a concept that is difficult to define. Examples: *Loyalty*, *justice* and *intelligence* are abstract nouns.

ACTIVE SENTENCE CONSTRUCTION – Sometimes called active voice. In active sentence construction the doer is the subject of the sentence. Example: Paul shot John. (See also passive sentence construction)

ACTIVE VOICE – See *active sentence construction*.

ADJECTIVE – An adjective is a word used to modify or give additional meaning to a noun or pronoun. Example: The *dirty* drunk passed out. (See also modify, modifier and adverb.)

ADJECTIVE CLAUSE – See *clauses*

ADVERB – An adverb is a word used to modify or give additional meaning to a verb, adjective or other adverb. Examples: He moved *quickly*. He moved *very quickly*.

ADVERB CLAUSE – See *clauses*

ANTECEDENT – The word or words preceding a pronoun to which the pronoun refers. Example: The sergeant expressed his confidence in us. (*Sergeant* is the noun to which *his* refers.)

APOSTROPHE – A punctuation mark ('). It is used to indicate an omitted letter or letters in a word or contraction. Example: He**'ll** do it again. The apostrophe is also used to form possessives. Examples: Carl**'s** pistol is broken. Dennis**'** pistol is not broken.

APPOSITIVE – A word, phrase or clause in opposition. An appositive renames a noun. Example: Our lieutenant, *a nice man*, was promoted.

ARTICLE – An article is a type of adjective. Examples: *A*, *an* and *the* are the most frequently used articles.

AUXILIARY VERB – A verb that precedes the main verb. Examples: *Has, have, had, could, would, may, might, must,* and *can* are some examples of auxiliary verbs.

CAPITALIZATION – In public safety report writing all letters are capitals

CASE – Case denotes the relation of nouns and pronouns to other words in a sentence. There are three cases. In the **nominative case** the noun or pronoun is the subject of a verb, or is an appositive to a subject noun or is a predicate noun. Examples: *Rodney* shot the pistol. (nominative case, subject of the verb) The shorter officer, Rodney, shot the pistol. (Rodney is in the nominative case, as an appositive to *officer*. The officer shooting the pistol is Rodney. (Rodney is in the nominative case because it is a predicate noun after the copulative verb *is* referring to officer.) The **possessive case** indicates possession. Example: I shot Rodney's pistol. The **objective case** indicates that a noun or pronoun received the action of the verb or that it is the object of a preposition. For example: Rodney shot the pistol. (object of *shot*) Shooting the *pistol* was easy. (object of the gerund *shooting*) Rodney drove to the range to shoot. (object of the preposition *to*)

CHRONOLOGICAL ORDER – Arranged in the order of occurrence

CLAUSES – Clauses are groups of words that have subjects and finite verbs. Clauses may be able to stand be themselves as sentences or may be parts of sentences. An **independent clause** can stand by itself as a sentence. Example: Who did it?
There are three kinds of **dependent clauses**. Dependent clauses cannot be sentences by themselves. They are groups of words functioning as nouns or modifiers in sentences. **Noun clauses** are groups of words functioning as nouns. Example: How he escaped was stated in the report. **Adjective clauses** are groups of words functioning as adjectives. Example: A man I know grows marijuana plants that never flower. **Adverb clauses** are groups of words functioning as adverbs. Example: He was bitter that she deserted him.

COLLECTIVE NOUN – A word for more than one person or thing considered as a whole. Examples; Mob, gang and jury are collective nouns.

COLON – The colon (:) is used for the following: to separate clauses of a compound sentence joined by coordinating conjunction, to separate clauses of a compound sentence joined by a coordinating conjunction, to separate an interjection or other introductory element from the rest of a sentence, to enclose nonrestrictive phrases, to separate items in addresses and dates, to prevent misreading.

COMMA SPLICE (COMMA FAULT) – A comma splice occurs when two complete sentences are incorrectly joined together with a comma.

COMMON NOUN – A word for a person, place or thing of a general class.

COMPARATIVE ADJECTIVE – Adjectives have positive, comparative and superlative forms or degrees of comparison. Examples:

Positive	*Comparative*	*Superlative*
small	smaller	smallest
good	better	best
beautiful	more beautiful	most beautiful

COMPARATIVE ADVERBS – Adverbs have positive, comparative and superlative forms or degrees or degrees of comparison. Examples:

Positive	*Comparative*	*Superlative*
quickly	more quickly	most quickly

COMPLEX SENTENCE – See *sentence*.

COMPOUND-COMPLEX SENTENCE – See *sentence*.

COMPOUND SENTENCE – See *sentence*.

CONJUNCTION – Conjunctions are words used to join other words or groups of words. **Coordinating conjunctions** such as *and, but* and *or* connect words or phrases. So do **correlating conjunctions,** but they come in pairs: *either...or; neither...nor; both... and; not only...also.* **Subordinating conjunctions** join dependent and independent clauses. *As, as if, because, before, since, that, when, where* and *unless* are subordinating conjunctions.

CONTRACTION – A shortened word using an apostrophe to indicate the missing letter or letters. Example: *Aren't* is a contraction for *are not.* Contractions are informal and should not be used in public safety report writing except where necessary to quote a person.

COORDINATING CONJUNCTION – See *conjunction*.

COPULATIVE VERB – See *verb*.

CORRELATING CONJUNCTION – See *conjunction*.

DANGLING MODIFIER – A modifier that is not logically connected to the word it is modifying.

DEGREES OF COMPARISON – See *comparative adjective* and *comparative adverb*.

DEMONSTRATIVE PRONOUN – A demonstrative pronoun points out particular persons, places or thing. Example: *These* need to be replaced.

DEPENDENT CLAUSE – See *clause*.

EXCLAMATION POINT (EXCLAMATION MARK) (!) – is used after an exclamatory word or phrase to indicate surprise, anger or other strong emotion. Example: Aha! I caught you!

FIRST PERSON – See *person*.

FUTURE PERFECT TENSE – See *verb tenses*.

FUTURE TENSE – See *verb tenses*.

GERUND – A present participle ending in –ing and functioning as a noun. Examples: *Shooting* was his favorite hobby. Former officer Green enjoyed *drinking* in bars.

GERUND PHRASE – See *phrase*.

HELPING VERB – See *auxiliary verb*.

HOMONYM – A word which has the same pronunciation as another but with a different meaning. Examples: To, too, two.

HYPHEN – The hyphen (-) is used in public safety report writing to break a word between syllables at the end of a line of writing. The hyphen should be used sparingly. It is generally better to put an entire word on one line.

INDEFINITE PRONOUN – An indefinite pronoun refers to persons, places or things in a non-specific manner. Example: *Both* suspects confessed.

INFINITIVE – A verb form beginning with the word to and often functioning as a noun. Example: He likes *to run* for exercise.

INTERJECTION – An exclamation thrown in without grammatical connection. Example: Ouch!

INTRANSITIVE VERB – See *verb*.

MISPLACED MODIFIER – A misplaced modifier occurs when words in a sentence are in the wrong order. This causes the modifier to appear to modify a word other than that which was intended.

MODIFIER – Both adjectives and adverbs are modifiers. They modify other words in sentences by telling us more about those other words. Examples: The car is *green*. (adjective) He ran *quickly*. (adverb)

MODIFY – To limit in meaning or qualify. Adjectives modify nouns and pronouns. Adverbs modify verbs, adjectives and other adverbs.

NOMINAL – A noun-like word.

NOMINATIVE CASE – See *case*.

NOMINATIVE PRONOUN – The subject of a clause or sentence or a predicate nominative. Also known as subject pronoun. Examples: *Who* is calling? (subject) The victim was *he*. (predicate nominative)

NONRESTRICTIVE PHRASE – A phrase which can be removed from a sentence without altering the basic idea of the sentence. Example: The judge, *a former public safety officer*, is the best jurist around.

NOUN – A word for a person, place or thing. (See also abstract noun)

NOUN CLAUSE – See *clause*.

NOUN PHRASE – A noun and its modifiers. Examples: *A hurried and nervous burglar* makes mistakes. *The industrial part of town* was a high crime area.

OBJECTIVE CASE – See *case*.

OBJECTIVE PRONOUN – Usually a direct or indirect object or the object of a preposition. Examples: He hit *her*. (direct object) I told *him* my badge number. (indirect object) This if for *you* and *me*. (object of a preposition)

PARENTHESES – In public safety report writing, parentheses () are used to enclose clarifying information in a sentence. Example: He ran 200 yards (about a block). Because only essential information belong in a public safety report, parentheses should only be used when the information enclosed by them clarifies the meaning of a sentence.

PARTICIPAL PHRASE – See *phrase*.

PARTICIPLE – A verb form used as adjective. Example: The *stabbing* victim died.

PASSIVE SENTENCE CONSTRUCTION – Sometimes referred to as passive voice. In passive sentence construction the doer is the object of the sentence. Passive sentences usually use the word *by* to identify the doer. Example: John was shot by Paul.

PASSIVE VOICE – See *passive sentence construction*.

PAST PARTICIPLE – A participle (used usually with an auxiliary verb) to indicate a time gone by or a state completed in the past. Example: The marijuana *had grown* well.

PAST PERFECT TENSE – See *verb tenses*.

PAST TENSE – See *verb tenses*.

PERIOD – A period (.) is used to mark the end of a sentence or abbreviation.

PERSON – Person is a way of distinguishing verbs. In public safety report writing the writer should use the first person (I, me my, mine) when referring to himself/herself. Examples: I took the witness' statement. (first person) She said she lost everything. (third person)

PERSONAL PRONOUN – Refers to the person who is speaking or writing. Examples: I, my and me are personal pronouns.

PHRASES – Phrases are groups of words that do not have a subject and finite verb. A **prepositional phrase** is a preposition followed by a nominal. Example: *Stop at the red light*. A **participial phrase** begins with a present or past participle. It modifies a noun or pronoun. Example: *Holding the suspect by his arm*, the officer refused to let go. A **gerund phrase** is a participle phrase that functions as a nominal. Example: *Using profane language* is not permitted in public safety reports. A **noun phrase** is a phrase functioning as a noun. Example: The two geldings and one mare in *the lower field which had not been mowed* were stolen. A **verb phrase** is a main verb and its auxiliary verb(s).

POSITIVE FORM – See *comparative adjective* and *comparative adverb*.

POSSESSIVE PRONOUN – Used in place of nouns that are possessed or possess something. Examples: *My* pistol is loaded. The stolen goods are *his*.

PREDICATE – The predicate is what is being said about the topic of the sentence. It always contains a verb.

PREDICATE NOMINATIVE – A noun used after a copulative verb.

PREFIX – A syllable or group of syllables attached to the beginning of a word to alter its meaning. Example: A *non*-profit organization.

PREPOSITION – A connection word that connects a noun, pronoun or noun phrase to another sentence element such as a verb, a noun or an adjective. Examples: *In, by, for, with, to* and *from* are some prepositions.

PREPOSITIONAL PHRASE – See *phrase*.

PRESENT PARTICIPLE – A participle of present meaning. Example: *Running* water.

PRESENT PERFECT TENSE – See *verb tenses*.

PRONOUN – A word used in place of or as a substitute for a noun. For cases of pronouns, see *nominative pronoun*, *objective pronoun* and *possessive pronoun*. For types of pronouns, see *personal pronoun*, *relative pronoun*, *demonstrative pronoun* and *indefinite pronoun*.

PROPER NOUN – A word for a particular person, place or thing. Proper nouns usually begin with capital letters. Examples: San Diego, Saturday and Easter are proper nouns.

PUNCTUATION – See *period*, *comma*, *apostrophe*, *quotation mark*, *colon*, *semicolon*, *exclamation point*, *parentheses* and *hyphen*.

QUOTATION MARK – Quotation marks (") are used to enclose direct quotes and to enclose the titles of divisions and chapters of books and periodicals.

RELATIVE PRONOUN – Connects other words and generally comes before a verb in a sentence. Examples: The pistol, *which* was engraved, was stolen. I remember the description of the suspect *who* robbed the liquor store.

RUN-ON SENTENCE – A run-on sentence consists of two complete sentences incorrectly contained in one sentence and usually connected with the words *and*, *or*, or *but*.

SEMICOLON – The semicolon (;) is used in compound sentences between independent clauses not joined by connective words and in compound sentences between independent clauses joined by conjunctive adverbs. It is generally not appropriate to use in public safety reports.

SENTENCE – A sentence contains a complete thought with a subject and a predicate. A simple sentence is an independent clause. A compound sentence has two or more independent clauses. A complex sentence has an independent clause and one or more dependent clauses. A compound-complex sentence has two or more independent clauses and one or more dependent clauses.

SENTENCE FRAGMENT – A sentence fragment is an incomplete sentence presented as a sentence.

SIMPLE SENTENCE – See *sentence*.

SUBJECT – A subject of a sentence is usually a noun or pronoun and its modifiers. It is the topic of the sentence.

SUBORDINATING CONJUNCTION – See *conjunction*.

SUFFIX – A syllable or group of syllables added to the end of a word to change its meaning. Example: He walk*ed* a mile.

SUPERLATIVE FORM – See *comparative adjective* and *comparative adverb*.

SYLLABLE – A word or a part of a word produced with a single, uninterrupted sound.

TENSE CONSISTENCY – Tense consistency refers to the idea of keeping the same tense throughout the length of the sentence, paragraph or entire narrative.

TENSES – See *verb tenses*.

THIRD PERSON – See *person*.

TRANSITIVE VERB – See *verb*.

VERB – A word or group of words which usually express action or a state of being. (existence) A **finite verb** works with the subject to give a complete statement. Example: The documents had *compromised* him. A **non-finite verb** works as a nominal or modifier. Example: The *compromising* documents were incriminating. A **transitive verb** requires an object to complete its meaning. Example: The bullet *struck* the victim. An **intransitive verb** requires no object. Example: He *jogs* daily. A **copulative verb** is a kind of intransitive verb which connects the subject to a noun, pronoun or adjective in the predicate. Example: Joey Bingo is the lieutenant. (*is* connects Joey Bingo to *lieutenant*.)

VERB PHRASE – See *phrase*

VERB TENSES – Verbs indicate time through the use of tenses. **Present tense**: I *am writing* the report. **Past tense**: I *wrote* the report. **Future tense**: I *will write* the report. **Present perfect tense**: I *have written* the report. **Past perfect tense**: I *had written* the report. **Future perfect tense**: I *will have written* one hundred reports by the end of the month.